Seeing What Isn't There

DAVE—
Thanks for your
LEADERSHIP!

Bruce Jim

Seeing What Isn't There

A Leader's Guide to Creating Change in a Complex World

BRUCE LARUE & JIM SOLOMON

Deeds Publishing | Atlanta

This book is dedicated to all who desire to create a better future by learning to See What Isn't There.

Contents

How I See The World

"The only thing worse than being blind
is having sight but no vision."
Helen Keller

Let me tell you how I see the world. I have been legally blind since I was a young boy. I can recall just beginning to learn to read when my outer world of vision grew dim. From that time forward, I was unable to see detail such as the printed word.

Through a combination of focused intention and the *neuroplasticity*[1] of the human brain, what I could not see with my outer eyes, I learned to conceive with my mind's eye. I now help leaders see a future yet to be born, channeling the collective energy of others to make it a reality. This results in leaders seeing their own world differently, changing both themselves and the organizations they lead.

Because traditional employment was out of reach, I had to forge a different path. I started my own businesses, achieved a Ph.D., became a graduate school professor, and I now coach, lecture, and teach leaders around the world on leading change.

While I was unable to serve my own country in the military, I am privileged to advise leaders in the U.S. Department of Defense, including Army commanders. While I am not an engineer, I have worked with many top engineers on highly complex initiatives within global high-tech organizations. While I never led a city or government agency, I have advised many of those who do. I now serve as President of Chambers Bay Institute, where our mission is to build leaders who can lead change in their organizations, their communities, and their countries.

My life and work are testimony to this time-honored truth: *To change the world, you must first change how you see the world.*

Losing My Sight and Gaining My Vision

As early as age seven, the center of my retina, or *macula*, had largely deteriorated, leaving my peripheral vision mostly intact. This had a tremendous impact on how I see the world, both physically and cognitively. The macula is responsible for perceiving detail and color. The peripheral area around the macula, on the other hand, sees the world as an integrated whole, detecting patterns and movements.

I have learned to see the world more as an integrated whole rather than a collection of independent parts. Seeing patterns of connections between thoughts and ideas has helped me to understand the world in terms of systems of complex interdependencies. Much like the challenges and crises we face today, they cannot be seen in isolation nor solved independently of one another. Instead, in our communities, at work, and in society, we need leaders who can build coalitions of people to create change in our complex world. In short, we need Integrator Leaders.

Learning to See What Isn't There

Great leaders lead change; that is, they don't simply react to change—they create it. Throughout history, these leaders seem to have a unique ability to see what isn't there, and to inspire others with their vision to create the greatest achievements of our time. My question is always this: how do these exceptional leaders captivate the imagination of others to organize toward a common purpose? This question has become *the* focus of my life and career, and it is a quest I share with my business partner and co-author, Jim Solomon.

After retiring as an Army Colonel, Jim served in various executive leadership positions in the private sector. From his beginning as an Eagle Scout and member of the Corps of Cadets at the University of North Georgia,[2] Jim focused his career on developing leaders.

While he grew up in the suburbs of Washington, DC, it was his time in the Blue Ridge and Smoky Mountains that taught Jim to see the world differently. Whether hiking for pleasure or training as a soldier in this beautiful yet rough terrain, Jim learned valuable lessons about the dynamics of working with teams in both favorable and challenging conditions. One lesson was that the best leaders are those who influence the team rather than dictate to them. Another was that, while climbing to the top of the mountain may be a worthwhile goal, any enduring accomplishment is all about *WE, not ME.*

On 9/11, the hijackers struck the office Jim once occupied at the Pentagon, killing many of his colleagues. This deeply affected how he saw the world, reigniting his commitment to develop a new generation of capable leaders.

Our common interest in developing leaders allowed us to draw from one another's deep experience to create Chambers Bay Institute. Today, our certified team of consultants are involved in training and developing thousands of leaders across a wide range of organizations around the world. The lessons we have learned through our combined decades of experience and research serve as the basis of the book you are reading.

As you will see in the pages ahead, whether you are launching a strategic initiative, improving procedures, creating an Internal Development Path for your workers, reinforcing your cyber defenses, building a new urban center, or rebooting your country, leadership is about leading change. Leading must involve change, since maintaining the status quo would mean going backwards as others evolve around you, leaving you, your organization—and perhaps your entire society—behind.

What you are about to read is a proven and highly adaptive method for integrating and aligning the efforts of others to achieve shared goals. We sincerely hope this book will help you see your own world in new ways.

Bruce LaRue, Ph.D.
Chambers Bay, Washington

CHAPTER ONE

The View From The Canopy

"When you change the way you look at things,
the things you look at change."
Max Planck

Don was the Vice President of National Operations for one of the nation's largest wireless telecom companies.[3] His team of directors and their personnel were responsible for the maintenance and operation of the entire wireless network. Their Network Operations Control Center looked like a scene from NASA Mission Control. They worked under a spotlight in the hot seat.

While his team of directors was very competent individually, they tended to be highly reactive, and their supporting organizations did not always work well together. As we will explore in more detail later, Bruce (and his former partners)[4] advised Don and his team on the deployment of their 3G (third-generation) network, the backbone of today's smartphone platform. This highly complex initiative involved the development of an entirely new all-digital network and a corresponding overhaul of their internal organization.

While we knew that what we were doing was revolutionary,

none of us could have imagined how the convergence of wireless telecommunications, computing, and the internet would transform the daily lives of people around the world.

Avoiding the Brushfire Syndrome

While Don's team was excited about their mission, the task was overwhelming. Maintaining the existing network infrastructure was challenging enough, and they simply did not feel that they had the operational bandwidth to focus on their new strategic priority.

The first challenge was one of perspective. Don's organization was so busy reacting to problems and putting out continual brushfires on the jungle floor of their operation that they could not see through the smoke to address the true causes of these fires, let alone focus on their new initiative.

This *brushfire syndrome* became a vicious cycle, causing wide-scale burnout in the organization. The worse things became, the more Don felt he had to actively *manage* his team. This in turn made his team feel that Don did not trust them, and that he was micromanaging their operations, creating a downward spiral in morale and performance.

Building Ownership in Your Teams

Using techniques such as the Mini-Town Hall[5] and Action Teams, which we will discuss later in this book, we helped Don and his team to get off the jungle floor and into the canopy of their operation, giving them a clear line of sight to their goal. From this vantage point, we helped Don systematically engage with his directors and their teams in a way that no one had experienced before. Rather than focusing on *managing his people*, we helped Don to sketch a vision of the future for his team to complete and make their own.

Soon, his directors and their teams began to self-organize to design and deploy the new smartphone platform, creating a virtually seamless transition for their customers—all done in ways they had never imagined possible.

Don's team and their personnel learned to work cross-functionally, develop new processes, and to cross-train one another on all key aspects of the new operation. They learned to repeat this process, applying it to other objectives, and discovered newfound successes for their customers. They started looking forward to coming to work and developed a personal sense of responsibility and dedication toward their fellow teammates. A sense of pride and ownership began to take root in the teams, as it was evident they did not want to let each other down or let the initiative fail.

Because of this extraordinary team work, many earned significant promotions. Some of our biggest initial critics told us that the entire process forever changed how they *see themselves as leaders* and as a result, it forever changed how they lead their organizations. Don and his team didn't know it at the time, but they were all learning to become *Integrator Leaders.*[6]

Why We Need Integrator Leaders

Integrator Leaders possess the unique ability to *see what isn't there*, channeling the collective energy of others to make their vision a reality. Simply stated, *leadership is about leading change.* Rather than engaging in futile attempts to manage, adapt to, or resist change, Integrator Leaders help their teams to build a future yet to be born.

Change has become so pervasive that simply to survive means that we must learn to leverage change to our advantage by building organizations that are more adaptive, agile, creative, and innovative. Improving your change strategy by becoming an Integrator Leader is therefore not only a matter of survival, but it is the key to thriving in an increasingly volatile and uncertain world.

Globalization and automation are accelerating at a dizzying pace, leaving people, organizations, and whole societies struggling to adapt. Work is increasingly specialized, and specialization without integration leads to internal fragmentation, which is the enemy of any strategy. This is why we need Integrator Leaders capable of inspiring others with fresh visions of the future, coalescing and aligning the efforts of others to accomplish their mission.

In the pages ahead, you will learn to see change, not as something to be avoided or managed, but rather leveraged to your advantage.

Integrator Leader Reflections

- How can you help your own team become less reactive and more proactive in the face of change?

- How can you help your team move from compliance to commitment?

- How can you get your team to transition from taking orders to taking ownership?

CHAPTER TWO

Changing How We See Change

"Humans don't simply adapt to their environment; they
adapt their environment to themselves."
Bruce LaRue

At the most basic level, nature teaches us that organisms that
sense and adapt to changes in their environment will succeed,
while those that don't will fail. Organizations, like organisms,
must learn to sense and appropriately adapt to changes in their
environment to survive and thrive. Yet biological adaptation,
while crucial to our survival, is only part of the picture. Biological adaptation can be exceedingly slow and, at its root, largely
unconscious and reactionary.

Reactionary change is a form of change that *reacts* to symptoms rather than addressing underlying systemic causes. It is
impulsive rather than methodical and systemic, like plugging
your fingers in a leaking dike without realizing that the dike is
already breached upstream. Humans are renowned for this form
of myopic, sub-optimized behavior. We fail to look systemically,
to take in the big picture, and to understand how our actions
cause ripple effects throughout the world around us.

Reactionary change makes us feel better in the short term,

as though we have taken actions that will fix the problem. This form of change creates a false sense of security and complacency about the true dangers that may be approaching. That is, we may have plugged the holes in the dike surrounding our community, but despite our efforts, the breach upstream means that disaster is approaching.

How Humans Adapt Their Environment to Themselves

Humans are unique among other species on earth in that we don't simply adapt to our environment, but instead we adapt our environment to ourselves. This means that we are fundamentally and inextricably involved in creating and re-creating the world around us through the mechanism of culture. Humans have not yet learned to fully comprehend the second and third order effects of the changes that we ourselves initiate in the world.

How we respond to change is ultimately a choice. We can see change as a threat to be avoided or a challenge to be overcome. We can choose to be a victim to our circumstance, or we can learn to leverage change to our advantage. The key is to never surrender our ability to choose how we respond to our situation. This is the essence of how humans adapt, develop, and evolve, and it is what distinguishes us from nearly every other creature on this planet.

"The World Has Turned VUCA and This Changes Everything"

These were the words Major General (Retired) Robert Ivany, former Commandant of the U.S. Army War College,[7] would say as he and Bruce would write and present together in the years following the events of 9/11. VUCA, an acronym for "Volatile, Uncertain, Complex, and Ambiguous,"[8] means that our previous notions of predictability and control no longer apply. Small changes in a VUCA world can generate effects that intensify in unpredictable ways over space and time. It is a world that is far more volatile and uncertain than ever, driven primarily by unprecedented levels of interdependence and rapid change among actors and events. Small changes in such a complex system can cause ripple effects that amplify unpredictably over space and time, and often at dizzying speeds. Increased ambiguity makes it difficult, if not impossible, to project future outcomes based on past trends.

More than ever, we all need to learn how to adapt and thrive in a VUCA world. Clearly, this includes having a resiliency plan to prepare ourselves, our families, our organizations, and our communities for the VUCA challenges ahead. However, as you will learn to see in the next section, many of the challenges you face also pose hidden opportunities for change and transformation.

Rebooting Iceland: How a Nation Self-Organized to Rebuild Their Country

In the fall of 2008 just after the onset of the Great Recession, Bruce received a call from his doctoral student, Bjarni Snæbjörn Jónsson, an Icelander with a keen intellect and quiet, observant demeanor. Bjarni had a brilliant insight. He wanted to focus his doctoral dissertation on developing a process to help his nation recover from the worst financial calamity in its history. Further, he wanted to create a model for large-scale social change that could help other nations, organizations, and communities redefine their own future. He asked Bruce to serve as the Chair of his dissertation committee, becoming a fascinating odyssey for Bjarni's team of collaborators and the nation of Iceland.[9]

The 2008 global financial meltdown could have caused a similar meltdown in Icelandic society. Instead, a self-organizing group of 12 collaborators, referring to themselves as The Anthill, initiated two large National Assembly events, both of which spawned hundreds of smaller collaborative events composed largely of ordinary Icelandic citizens, culminating in the rewriting of the Icelandic Constitution.

This small nation state of 320,000 people is geographically three times the size of the Netherlands. It has all the infrastructure and institutions of a modern democracy and a documented history from the time of its settlement. As such it constitutes a fascinating microcosm, demonstrating how human social systems behave and adapt to the volatility, uncertainty, complexity and ambiguity of our modern world.

The Icelandic people are no strangers to hardship, but nothing prepared them for the series of compounding crises they faced following the financial meltdown of September 2008. With the help of the Gallup organization, The Anthill organizers intentionally brought together a cross-section of 1,200 participants from across Icelandic society in one room for the first major National Assembly event. The first part of the event was devoted to discussing the question, "What core values will guide us in developing our society and what is the purpose and future vision of the Icelandic nation?" The second major part of the event was devoted to the question, "What kind of future do we wish to co-create for generations to come?"

The dialogue produced a vast array of responses that were processed in real time using specialized software to create patterns and categories relating to different facets of society, such as welfare, health, environment, energy, justice, education, and business. The results were displayed in real time on a large digital display for all to see in the convention hall. The ensuing dialogue focused on how each of these societal systems could be engineered to manifest the values and aspirations defined in the first part of the meeting. Instead of feeling lost or hopeless in the face of the economic meltdown, the National Assembly process generated great excitement, and a means of channeling the anger and frustration of a nation into meaningful action toward a new future.

In the following months, core participants, as well as thousands of others, engaged in smaller collaborative dialogue sessions. Using principles and techniques similar to those we are exploring in this book, these self-organizing citizen groups focused on specific priorities identified within the inaugural National Assembly event.

The success of the first event led to a decision by the Icelandic Parliament to organize a second National Assembly to initiate a major rewriting of the Icelandic Constitution. Since then, thousands have continued to contribute to the process using a remarkable, simple and transparent set of strategies for facilitating dialogue and collaborative web-based tools and technologies. The process developed for the Iceland National Assembly has become a model for use in scores of large and small social change efforts across the country and beyond, many of which are ongoing at the time of this writing.

In a televised interview broadcast nationwide in advance

of the first Iceland National Assembly, Bruce encouraged the people of Iceland to look forward to a new future, not to waste their energy either laying blame for the 2008 catastrophe or attempting to return to some elusive golden time in the past. He cautioned the Icelandic people not to become overly reactionary. When in crisis mode, we tend to expend our effort and precious resources trying to plug one hole in the dike after another, only to find that a dozen more spring up around us. This causes panic and frustration while failing to address the underlying cause of the catastrophe and creating an effective long-term response.

As we learn to respond to the VUCA world unfolding all around us, we must focus our energy on forging an effective longer-term path forward rather than only dealing with immediate crises. We must ensure that our short-term measures are in alignment with our longer-term vision and strategy and that we are focusing on the future rather than trying to return to the past.

VUCA events often reveal weaknesses in the core systems that support our hyper-connected society. For example, we can see this in the over-speculation on Wall Street leading to the collapse of Lehman Brothers in 2008, triggering a global financial crisis. Another example is the 2010 Japanese earthquake and tsunami which led to the Fukushima nuclear meltdown. Catastrophic failures of our infrastructure and core institutions of society caused by natural and man-made disasters continue unfolding all around us, and our growing interdependence means that a single event can result in a cascade of unforeseen consequences.

For many organizations today, VUCA events often include the rise of an unexpected competitor, disruptive technology, or innovative product that suddenly upends their competitive advantage. These organizations, and the people within them, often become victims of their own successes, trapped within what we call the *prison of the known*. [10] That is, leaders in these organizations often mistakenly assume that what made them successful in the past is also their formula for the future. Rather than questioning these basic assumptions, when faced with VUCA challenges, the same organizations will double down on the now outmoded strategies that made them successful in the past, all but assuring their demise.

Some VUCA challenges are *slow-burning* and, therefore, especially insidious. This is due in part to the lag between cause and effect. Cause and effect within complex systems aren't linear processes, but cyclical and self-reinforcing. Changes in one part of the system often cause changes in other parts and magnify over time. Given the hyper-connected nature of our world, traditional notions of control simply no longer apply.

If we look *the right way*, we can see profound opportunities that emerge from VUCA challenges. As we see with the example of Iceland, small changes in the right places within a complex adaptive system can have tremendous positive ripple effects. We have witnessed hundreds of examples over time, where leaders have successfully transformed organizational challenges into opportunities for their people to learn, develop, and innovate, all in service of their mission. To do this, we must learn to see beyond the barrage of events that cloud our vision and compete for our limited attention by using the principles of Soft Focus.

The Art of Soft Focus

Rather than wasting precious energy on futile attempts to control events in a VUCA world, Integrator Leaders use *Soft Focus,* [11] or a finely-tuned form of peripheral vision, to scan for threats and opportunities that others miss.

We have been conditioned to focus on particular events at the expense of recognizing the patterns that give rise to them. Pattern recognition is more vital today than ever. We too often fail to see how our individual actions, amplified over time and space by the multitudes of others behaving the same way, can lead to unforeseen and sometimes disastrous results.

Most people vacillate between states of hyper-focus and constant distraction, where they either tune out the world around them in order to focus or become unable to focus at all. Attention requires energy, which is a finite resource. To the extent our attention is fragmented and focused on details, we narrow our field of vision and, hence, our realm of possibility. [12]

It is far too easy to be seduced into equating activity with progress. As the military knows all too well, tactical decisions have strategic consequences. This means that we all must learn to see our actions within a broader context. Unless we recognize how our actions relate to the whole, we risk making short-term decisions that run counter to our long-term values and goals.

Soft Focus is a discipline that informs decisions through a broader view, ensuring that today's choices take you where you want to be tomorrow. Soft Focus helps to recognize patterns in events and determine where to leverage your efforts. It teaches you not to become too wedded to your favorite scripts, or to allow your vision or goals to become blinders that prevent you from identifying new opportunities and fresh alternatives for action.

As a former squadron commander and Navy test pilot, Linda Shaffer-Vanaria realizes more than most that fixating on details can get you killed. She said "As a fighter pilot, you can't become hard-focused on one thing, you must remain aware of your environment in its totality at all times. A constant barrage of information must remain within your scan—pilot jargon for keeping a strategically timed eye on everything important. You must connect all of these dots and hold the big picture in focus in real time."

Mastery of Soft Focus requires honed skills, developed intuition, and a heightened state of mind. As an Integrator Leader, consider adopting the following practices:

1. **Focus on Your Mission:** This allows the critical attention items and details to stand out naturally and helps you to prioritize your activities in the moment.

2. **Scan Your Environment Strategically:** A strategic scan helps maintain the Soft Focus required to remain aware of the big picture, while identifying where to focus your attention.

3. **Recognize Patterns:** Soft Focus turns your attention to patterns rather than details and allows you to naturally develop intuitive awareness.

4. **Focus on What, Not How:** Develop skill and muscle memory in your chosen field so you are not hard-focused on "how to fly" but rather on where you are going.

5. **Develop Contextual Awareness:** See your circumstances and actions in the context of the whole, and in alignment with your mission.

6. **Take Time to Reflect:** Allow time for mindful reflection and creative imagination daily.

Soft Focus can help you locate hidden patterns in the barrage of events you face daily to gain maximum leverage from your choices. Next, we will learn more about what it takes to become an Integrator Leader, learning how to use the principles of Soft Focus to scan your environment and locate high-leverage points for change. We will then show you how to conduct a similar process with your entire team using what we call the Mini-Town Hall.

Integrator Leader Reflections

- Are you leading change or reacting to it?

- What VUCA challenges are you and your organization facing, and how can you transform these challenges into opportunities?

- How can you use the principles of Soft Focus to see patterns and identify high leverage points for change in the world around you?

CHAPTER THREE

Becoming An Integrator Leader

"The art of leadership is influencing others and
organizations to accomplish a task or mission."

**James L. Terry, Lieutenant General
U.S. Army, Retired**

Integrator Leaders create a clear compass heading for their team
while helping them develop the map to get from here to there.
Integrator Leaders understand that they must *lead through influence* and coordinate with other teams to create alignment behind
their organization's strategic goals. In this way, they serve as the
initial *string that connects the pearls*, forging new bonds of influence between functional groups, enabling teams to self-organize
behind the mission.

As Albert Einstein reminds us, "We cannot solve our problems with the same thinking we used when we created them."
Integrator Leaders help their team see their world through new
eyes and to use challenges as crucibles for learning, growth, and
development. They know this can have tremendous positive
ripple effects across an entire organization, leading to superior
outcomes for customers and a work environment that attracts,
develops, and retains top talent.

While the industrial age ushered in forms of management predicated on precision, predictability, and control, these strengths have in many ways become our weakness, giving way to a premium on speed, adaptability, and flexibility. Rather than attempting to maintain some elusive state of stability, Integrator Leaders help their organizations leverage change to their competitive advantage.

Great leaders lead change; that is, they don't simply react to change—they create it. What drove these leaders forward? How did they inspire others with their vision of the future? Why did some of their efforts succeed while others failed? How can we help people to stop resisting or simply reacting to change occurring around them, and instead develop and work toward a new vision for the future? How can we harness the forces of change to our benefit to make ourselves, our organizations, and our societies more resilient?

Seeing a New City — Before It's There

In its early days, University Place was an unincorporated region at the periphery of Pierce County in the southern Puget Sound region of Washington State. As his hometown, Bruce can attest that it had very good schools, a great view, and little else. It was largely a bedroom community, while its citizens often worked in places like Seattle 30 miles to the north and did most of their shopping and entertaining outside the city. This resulted in a nearly nonexistent sales tax base which compounded the city's revenue challenges and limited its capacity for development. Chances are University Place would have been largely left behind had it not been for the visionary work of two forward-thinking city managers, a progressive City Council, and dedicated staff.

The first of these city managers, Bob Jean, had been serving as a Board Member of the International City Managers Association (ICMA), a position which exposed him to the very best old and new cities around the world. Bob's goal was to bring the very best people and ideas together to help the City of University Place create a new downtown.

To help develop a vision for the future, Bob first took the council and key staff members to see other forward-looking communities around the country. Council and staff members were able to see what was possible elsewhere and gain an understanding of why they needed to abandon strip malls and suburban sprawl in favor of a walkable, transit-oriented, mixed-use design for their new town center.

The effort started while Bob was the City Manager and Steve Sugg served as his Assistant City Manager/Project Director. Bruce worked closely with Steve who continued the momentum, as Bob's successor as the City Manager. Steve was highly influenced early in life by developments such as the Country Club Plaza in Kansas City where he lived as a graduate student, and later the Pearl Street Mall in Boulder, Colorado, a beautiful, pedestrian-oriented downtown shopping district where his wife had lived.

Steve understood that to achieve the vision of a new and vibrant city-center, he needed to get the community to become involved in creating the vision. He also had to gain the buy-in from the city staff charged with implementing it. They had no idea at the time they would serve as stewards of the community's vision through two major national recessions and numerous transitions among council members, some of whom had agendas that conflicted with the long-term vision of the community.

Steve's initial job as City Manager was to refocus the entire city staff and their limited resources on their core PURPOSE: implementing the community's vision for a new downtown. To do this, he had to clearly articulate WHY an inordinate portion of the city's resources needed to be focused on this large and costly initiative—often at the expense of other popular programs.

Steve needed first to ensure that the citizens and staff understood the WHAT of their mission. That is, WHAT is the community's vision, WHAT are the key challenges faced with its implementation, and WHAT was at stake if they failed to make it a reality. Second, he had to help them understand WHY it would benefit everyone in the community to have a thriving downtown in their own backyard. He had to get the staff on board by helping them understand WHY success in this critical initiative would benefit them and their careers, too. This made it easier for him to focus everyone's efforts on making the necessary sacrifices to implement the vision.

To facilitate the development of the city's vision, Steve wisely invited Dan Burden, one of the country's leading experts on city redesign, to assist them. Dan is an internationally known expert and civic innovator, helping get the world *back on its feet*. Through his role as Director of Innovation and Inspiration at Blue Zones, he integrates street design, public safety, economic and land-use planning to envision healthy, active communities that are pedestrian-friendly and bicycle-friendly. Dan helps communities become places where people want to live and where businesses thrive.[13]

Dan is a consummate Integrator Leader, able to bring together a diverse set of stakeholders to focus on a common purpose. Using an approach very similar to the Mini-Town Hall described in this book, Dan brought together a broad array of citizen stakeholders in focus group sessions he calls *charrettes*. These are facilitated brainstorming sessions and citizen-driven design workshops in which local residents help with a hands-on approach to design solutions to their neighborhood problems, while creating a vision for the future of their community.

As he has done hundreds of times around the world, Dan helps everyone participating in this process to *see their community through new eyes,* falling in love with cities again. He helps people remember the best of their common heritage while focusing on a vision of the future.

Christened the Village at Chambers Bay, after the now world-famous Chambers Bay golf course just down the road, the new downtown now serves as the city's community and economic center, with miles of tree-lined walking paths leading to its mixed-use gathering place.

The excitement that has grown around this vision over time is reenergizing the community and staff to overcome any barriers they face to make it a reality. As a result, this city is transforming itself from a sleepy bedroom community to what is becoming a premier place to live, work, and play in the South Puget Sound.

Escaping the Prison of the Known

To take the idea of a new downtown from concept to reality, city leaders and staff needed to help the community *see* differently: to begin to see their town *as it could be* rather than how it was in the past. Many citizens were resistant, fighting against change.

Like many corporate, non-profit, and governmental agencies struggling to remain viable in the face of accelerating change today, they were stuck in the *prison of the known*. Bob and Steve were able to help the community escape the shackles of their past by developing a new vision for their future along with a compelling rationale as to WHY change was both necessary and desirable.

To focus the attention of your team on the future, you must first guide them out of the *prison of the known*. This prison is where our individual favored ways of seeing become *ways of not seeing*. If we are not careful, we see our future in terms of the past, which is a bit like driving a car by looking in the rearview mirror.

Yes, whether we realize it or not, most of us exist inside a prison of our own making. The walls of our prison cell can best be thought of as our basic assumptions. To become an Integrator Leader, you must first become self-aware, meaning that you clearly perceive your own basic assumptions and learn to consciously modify them where necessary.

Our current reality did not arise by chance. Rather, each of us exists within our own *prison of the known*, comprised of the preconceptions, assumptions, and biases that make up our world view. However, looked at another way, the same forces that have imprisoned us can also create new worlds limited only by our imagination [14] and collective will to act.

You may think that what makes you who you are is a given; but the *self* is largely a constructed entity, evidenced by the degree to which the concept of *self* changes across cultures. By first becoming self-aware, that is, becoming aware of the assumptions and biases that comprise the *self*, the Integrator Leader learns to see the subtle basic assumptions operating both internally and externally to their organization. This heightened intuitive sensitivity helps to better understand the complexities of a situation or what makes another person tick. With time and practice, you can learn to quickly grasp the basic assumptions operating within an individual or the culture of an organization.

Skilled Integrator Leaders can comprehend multiple points of view without being tied to any of them. This is the difference between *assumptions that hold us* and *assumptions we hold*. In other words, we all see the world through an unconscious set of beliefs and assumptions that hold us captive to some degree. They are a lens through which we evaluate everything without realizing we are wearing glasses.

Further, this prison grows into a self-reinforcing echo chamber through the effects of social media, marketers, and internet search engines that constantly feed us more of what we already believe and desire based on secret algorithms. Rather than becoming aware of and questioning the basic assumptions that drive us, our assumptions are being systematically manipulated and reinforced by the digital air we breathe, leading to the heightened social fragmentation and disintegration we see today.

Basic assumptions can be thought of as cultural DNA. Unlike biological DNA, your cultural DNA can be manipulated by others. If you have the courage to leave the familiarity of your own *prison of the known* and examine the hidden assumptions that stealthily guide your life, you can begin to intentionally change the lenses through which you see the world.

While many approaches to leadership development focus on changing behavior, we have found that we don't need to change a person's behavior. Instead, if we can help people to *see their world in new ways,* positive actions naturally follow. In other words, if you want to change the world, begin by *changing how you see the world.*

Avoiding the High Producer's Trap

The *High Producer's Trap* is one of the most common *prisons* holding leaders and their organizations captive today. This occurs when individuals are promoted into leadership because they have been very good at producing results. In our experience, the assumption many leaders mistakenly hold at this point is that what got me here (my strength as a producer) will get me where I want to go in becoming an effective leader. They further assume that they were put in charge because they were the smartest person in the room. Here is where the strength of the leader becomes their weakness.

An Integrator Leader's job is not to produce results. Rather, their job is to build teams and organizations that can self-organize to accomplish their mission—in effect becoming operational advisors and force multipliers for the leader. Further, unlike during industrial times, the knowledge-based organizations of today are composed mainly of knowledge workers who know more about their job than their boss. This means that the boss is rarely the smartest person in the room. One of our clients said it best: "If I'm the smartest person in the room, I'm in the wrong room."

In our earlier example, Don learned that while in the past, he may have been the technical expert, he needed to shift toward empowering his team of specialized experts to self-organize behind the mission. He learned that he could never again be, nor did he want to be, the smartest person in the room. Rather, he became known as a highly capable leader who earned trust and commitment from his team through his authentic style, his openness to feedback, and his ability to effectively incorporate input from his team into his decisions.

Leaders who try to maintain authority by attempting to be the smartest person in the room, are often the most insecure. To compensate, when they feel challenged, they are quick to remind everyone who's boss. These leaders tend to have difficulty recognizing and rewarding others' accomplishments, may try to limit information and communication flows within and between teams (creating knowledge silos), and frequently take credit for the ideas of others.

If allowed to go unchecked, these leaders create a dysfunctional culture of dependency where all roads lead to the boss's desk, effectively making the leader a single point of failure for the organization.

Those caught in the High Producer's Trap often feel threatened by people they perceive to be smarter than themselves, effectively becoming gatekeepers that chase away the best talent while dumbing down the team over time. The best people begin to feel increasingly disempowered as they realize that they cannot make decisions without the leader's consent and are unlikely to get credit, recognition, or rewards for their efforts. This creates a "salute and obey" culture rather than a climate of empowered and engaged workers.

Growing Beyond the Founder

Organizational founders often begin with a powerful and inspiring vision that attracts people to their cause. If it makes it through its early entrepreneurial stages, the organization goes through a set of predictable phases. At one critical juncture, the organization grows beyond the capacity of the founder to manage it. This leads to the founder exerting more control, thereby limiting the ability of the organization to grow.

At some level, the founder may know that they must let go of the operational rains by developing appropriate structures and processes, and delegating authority to others in the organization. Yet when things do not go according to their plan, the leader will often blame others for the failure and then take back control, thus putting in motion a vicious cycle referred to by Ichak Adizes as the *Founder's Trap*.[15] At this point, the founder becomes both the greatest asset and the biggest liability of the organization.

Companies stuck in the Founder's Trap often become targets for mergers and acquisitions by other firms. If the company manages to stay in business through this growth phase and has a good product or service, an acquiring firm is likely to sideline the founder to assure that he or she can no longer disrupt the operations of the firm.

Acquiring firms are often cash heavy aging organizations seeking new business opportunities. They will frequently bring in a more rigid structure and culture which tends to chase off the remainder of the best talent in the firm. This further saps the entrepreneurial spirit that once attracted top talent and made the firm successful.

In sum, regardless of your initiative and how powerful and compelling your original vision is, it is crucial that you begin your journey with these critical lessons in mind. Prepare in advance for how you will grow, keep your best people engaged, remain flexible in the face of change and shifting priorities, and learn how to create a culture that attracts, develops, and retains top talent.

Avoiding the Traps

Remaining in either the High Producer's Trap or the Founder's Trap can cause irreparable damage to the organization as—in both cases—your best talent leaves in search of better opportunities. The way to avoid these traps is to focus instead on becoming an Integrator Leader. As you learn to operate this way, your current job becomes easier as your team learns to self-organize behind your intent.

When we teach people to become Integrator Leaders, we bring out the very best in their people, too. This operational intelligence leads to a more innovative and productive workplace. Integrator Leaders believe they exist merely to help their team succeed. They become mentors and coaches to their staff, helping people learn to self-organize to accomplish mission objectives.

Integrator Leaders have high standards and a way of continually raising the bar that brings out the very best in people, who often surpass their expectations. And finally, Integrator Leaders realize that any recognition they receive comes as a direct result of helping their teams succeed. They take no credit for success themselves but constantly give it back to those around them, building a vital sense of trust and commitment within the team.

Next, we will briefly explore the core principles that guide the Integrator Leader, and in the following chapter, we will show you how to systematically apply these principles to lead change in your own organization.

Principles that Guide the Integrator Leader

Principle 1: Work Yourself Out of Your Job | As an Integrator Leader, make it your objective to work yourself out of your job. This is your fastest route to success. Many leaders try to make themselves indispensable—this leads to the High Producer's or Founder's Trap and should be avoided at all cost. Instead, you want to make your team less dependent upon you over time. Coach, mentor, give your team suggestions and guidance, but do not solve problems for them. Ultimately, you want your team to own the solution, rather than merely follow your orders.

Principle 2: Integrated Solutions Require Integrated Operations | Looking at your organization through the eyes of your customer, you must assume that customers don't necessarily want what you are selling. Yet, they cannot necessarily tell you exactly what they do want. Instead, what customers expect are integrated solutions to their problems. However, we can't create integrated solutions if we are fragmented internally; integrated solutions require integrated internal operations.

Principle 3: Focus on Outcomes Rather than Inputs | We must turn the mechanistic management paradigm inside-out. The industrial age paradigm focused on worker input rather than the outcomes achieved. Yet the only thing customers really care about is the outcome: that is, the products and services that they purchase. Too often, workers are expected to simply follow processes without analyzing and improving them. Unfortunately, standard operating procedures can become a substitute for thinking and innovation. We want people to be involved in continually refining the processes that they are expected to follow, and to be accountable for the outcomes they achieve.

Principle 4: From Command and Control to Strategic Intent
The most effective military leaders we work with focus on defining their intent, giving maximum latitude to front-line troops on how best to accomplish their mission. The U.S. Army refers to this as *Mission Command*[16] or moving from a system of rigid, top-down control to commanders viewing front-line troops as their eyes and ears on the ground and as their operational advisors.

Translating this to the civilian sector, the most effective leaders we work with today provide the *compass heading*, meaning that they set the priorities and the criteria by which they will judge a successful outcome. Employees then operate freely within appropriate left and right boundaries to create the roadmap for HOW to achieve the intended outcome.

Principle 5: Whole Systems Perspective | We too often think of the future in terms of the past. Favored ways of seeing become ways of not seeing. Individuals and functional groups become too myopic, failing to understand the big picture and what they need from one another for the operation as a whole to succeed. The team needs to view things from the canopy, so they don't get disoriented when they're on the jungle floor.

Principle 6: Ask—Don't Tell | To the greatest extent possible, you want the team to own the HOW; ownership is key to building a culture of commitment. As the legendary management consultant Peter Drucker said, "the leader of the past knew how to tell; the leader of the future will know how to ask." He was not referring to being polite, but rather acknowledging the fact that knowledge workers know more about their job than their boss. Therefore, *they must define the task.* That is, specialized knowledge workers hold the critical operational intelligence necessary to accomplish the mission.

Now that we have reviewed the principles that guide the Integrator Leader, it is time to put them into practice. Next, you will learn how to use our Change Integrator© model to help you transform your own vision for the future into reality.

Integrator Leader Reflections

- Are you setting the compass heading for your team with clear intent and rationale to guide their action?

- Are you operating at the helm or in the engine room?

- Are you focusing on WHAT and WHY while empowering your team to come up with HOW to get you there?

CHAPTER FOUR

The Change Integrator

"A great change leader creates other change leaders."
John Kotter

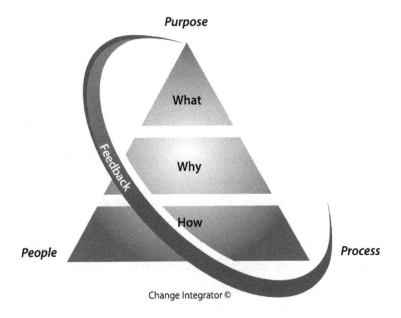

In this chapter, we will explore the Change Integrator model as a means of guiding your vision from concept to reality. As we can see from the Change Integrator model above, the first role of the integrator leader is to clarify PURPOSE (strategic intent) and to build a compelling rationale for WHY change is necessary. Once this is clear, the leader must engage their PEOPLE in HOW to develop the PROCESSES necessary to achieve the PURPOSE.

Begin with a focus on the PURPOSE (WHAT) that guides the change effort and the rationale (WHY). Then ask the team for input as to HOW best to accomplish the PURPOSE. The sequences are nearly always the same: WHAT, WHY, then ask HOW. That is, after providing the PURPOSE, ask the team for their input, their insights, what is working, and what is not; then help integrate what they have proposed into a course of action. Ultimately, we want to create teams that can self-organize behind your intent to accomplish their mission.

The FEEDBACK LOOP on the Change Integrator represents a constant real-time integration of strategy and action that goes both ways. It symbolizes the critical need to ensure that strategy is being informed by action, action is being informed by strategy, and that WHAT and HOW are always aligned. It symbolizes our ability to identify and exploit unforeseen opportunities and to spawn new innovations. The FEEDBACK LOOP also reminds us that tactical decisions have strategic consequences.

The role of the Integrator Leader is to guide, mentor, provide essential resources, and remove barriers to progress. The leader is also responsible for ensuring that the team operates within appropriate boundaries while achieving essential outcomes. Your job as a leader is ultimately to guide the ship from the helm and not from the engine room. That is, you set the compass heading and priorities while you help your team self-organize to create an ownership mentality in how they accomplish the mission.[17]

Throughout this process we must be careful to separate WHAT from HOW. That is, we want to keep our strategic intent separate from HOW this strategy is operationalized in practice. This is because the old strategic planning paradigm rooted in industrial times routinely attempted to control both the WHAT and HOW of change. This approach made sense in early industrial times when most companies focused on long runs of standardized products and services with very little variation. Today we must turn this paradigm inside out to create nimble, flexible organizations that can adapt and leverage change to their advantage.

Integrator Leaders and the Wireless Revolution

Kerry Larson was an Integrator Leader that had a front-row seat at the birth of the wireless revolution. His job, in a nutshell, was to take the ideas of one visionary man, Craig McCaw, and align and organize the company to make this vision a reality. McCaw Cellular would later be purchased by AT&T, becoming a key player in the smartphone industry that has since permeated modern life.

There are priceless lessons to be learned in this inside story of how an entire industry was born, survived the clash of two drastically different corporate cultures, and later achieved astounding success using many of the key principles we are exploring in this book.

The Art of Seeing What Isn't There

Try for just a moment to imagine a time before the smartphone. Believe it or not, most people felt that cellular telephones would never amount to anything. Investors were suspicious of the profits they were told could be made in the new industry and therefore remained largely on the sidelines. The world had just watched Motorola nearly go bankrupt deploying a satellite phone network. Despite the fact the two technologies were entirely different, investors painted cellular technology with the same broad technological brush. They were unwilling to commit to funding such a risky and unproven idea largely existing in the vision of one man: Craig McCaw.

McCaw was undeterred. Like all great visionary leaders, he *saw what wasn't there* and was determined to build a team that could make it reality. Seemingly against all odds, McCaw and his team successfully competed against the established regional telephone companies while somehow managing their burgeoning debt load. The company was soon growing rapidly across the country, acquiring properties and spectrum licenses. One of McCaw's favorite sayings was "flexibility is heaven." He despised bureaucracy and realized that creating a company of highly innovative and motivated knowledge workers was the only way to succeed.

McCaw's strategy was to hire very smart people, give them a clear sense of vision and purpose, and let them figure out the rest. Kerry's job was to build an organization capable of transforming Craig's vision into reality.

Kerry knew that as the company rapidly grew in geographic reach and technical complexity, new structures and systems would need to be developed, but they needed to be as flexible, scalable, and nimble as possible. As the strategic priorities of the organization changed, all the people and structures that support it must continually evolve. For Kerry, this meant actively listening to the people at the operational level and incorporating their input into the strategy:

> "We were not sure how best to market this new technology in the various parts of the country and compete with different regional competitors, so we let these smart people figure it out in their part of the country and share with the rest of us what worked and what didn't." [18]

Once acquired by AT&T, the two distinct corporate cultures enjoyed a productive, albeit brief, honeymoon. Soon, however, the more bureaucratic, highly structured, and slow-moving culture of AT&T clashed with the flatter, decentralized, and highly entrepreneurial culture of McCaw Cellular.

Admittedly, some elements of structure created under the new ownership helped the rapidly growing company streamline and rationalize some of its core processes. For example, under McCaw, the Network Operations Control Centers were regionalized, creating unnecessary redundancies and inconsistent approaches to managing what was becoming a single national wireless network. Under AT&T, these regional control centers were consolidated into one central location, thereby creating a consistent approach while significantly cutting costs.

However, some of the structural changes imposed by AT&T, along with key leadership changes, clearly eroded both the entrepreneurial spirit of McCaw and the company's ability to respond effectively to heightened competition and rapid technological change. AT&T broke the company into traditional functional areas such as Product Development, Marketing, IT, Engineering, and Operations. As new products and services were developed, each functional area was tasked according to its unique functional roles. Each functional area was then subjected to rigorous quality and financial metrics.

At one level, each of these structural and leadership changes made perfect sense. However, analyzed at another level, it quickly became clear that many of these functional areas began to work against one another because each was motivated by different rewards for performance.

For example, Product Development and Marketing were rewarded if they produced a rapid time-to-market, while Engineering and Operations were rewarded according to the quality and performance of the network. Conflicts emerged between these groups as new products and services were being rapidly introduced into the network with little regard to their impact on network operations, maintenance, and network bandwidth usage. The result was great fanfare around new product offerings that challenged the network to the extent that the customer experience suffered. At the same time, the explosive growth in popularity of wireless services challenged the company to keep up with demand for basic services, while continually introducing new offerings.

Predictably, the company under AT&T became very hierarchical and bureaucratic. Strict protocols of communication and control were introduced. Communication amongst individuals in various ranks in the hierarchy was strictly controlled. All strategic and many operational decisions were made at the top of the organization, with little or no input from those who would be affected by the change. Performance Improvement Teams were dismantled.

In short order, the organization went through a profound cultural change. The company became more ponderous and was unable to quickly respond to the rapid changes occurring in the industry.

Advancements in technology did not necessarily translate into satisfied customers. Highly skilled product development teams and engineers began to create scores of new services and gadgetry that, as it turned out, many customers rarely used or even knew existed. On a trip to demonstrate many of these new features and services to a major corporate client, one AT&T Wireless vice president remembers the CEO's response: "These features are indeed impressive. Now tell me how they will help me solve the myriad problems I face as I try to manage my global workforce." The VP, who was rarely short on words, was rendered nearly speechless. The customer did not want more features and services, but rather integrated solutions to his problems.

As in many traditional companies, each functional division began to operate as a fiefdom, fighting for more personnel and budget increases. No single consistent unifying vision and knowledge management system was in place to ensure that each functional area worked in concert with all others in furthering company strategy.

Building cross-functional alignment behind the design and deployment of their 3G (third-generation) network, therefore, became a major focus in the company's efforts to reinvent itself. All this was occurring at a time when the industry itself was undergoing a profound transformation due to the merging of telecommunications, computing, and the Internet.

Completing the Vision

At this juncture, Bruce joined Kerry[19] in advising several key leaders at AT&T Wireless on organizing the design and deployment of their 3G network, which became the smartphone platform we know today. Using many of the principles and techniques we are exploring in this book, they reached their goal of building an entirely new network platform in less than two years, an astounding accomplishment. This was followed by the most successful IPO in the history of Wall Street at the time.[20]

During their work together, Kerry would often say to Bruce: "Purpose—People—Process," forming a triangle with his hands signifying how PURPOSE guided everything else. This was almost a mantra for him. For Kerry, this meant that the support structures of an organization, its PEOPLE and PROCESSES, must self-organize to integrate and align behind its PURPOSE. This concept was foundational for Kerry, and it forms the underlying framework of the Change Integrator model.

Seeing the Operation Through the Eyes of Your Team

One of the primary goals of the Change Integrator model is to help leaders learn to see their organization through the eyes of their people, treating them as their operational advisors. Employees have typically been on the receiving end of change initiatives and are rarely asked for input or consulted along the way. Once we understand the true nature of knowledge work, we approach leadership and change in our organizations differently. Treat your workers as the eyes and ears of your operation.

Provide people with a clear strategic intent and rationale, and then *ask* them how best to get from here to there.

If you consistently utilize this form of leadership, your people will not only provide you with input on your course of action, they will learn to bring you an entire plan of action and *ask you for your input on their plan.* This is when you know you are on the right track. Your job should get easier while your people step up, take more initiative, engage with one another, and take ownership of HOW change is implemented.

In the following chapter, we will introduce you to the *Mini-Town Hall*, a unique process designed to help your team self-organize behind your intent to accomplish their mission, ultimately becoming your operational advisors.

Integrator Leader Reflections

- Are you providing a clear purpose and rationale for the direction of your organization?

- Are you treating your team as your operational advisors?

- How will you use the Change Integrator model in your role as a leader?

CHAPTER FIVE

The Mini-Town Hall

*"...skate to where the puck is going to be,
not to where it has been..."*
Wayne Gretzky

The *Mini-Town Hall* is a process we designed to help our clients become Integrator Leaders in their own organization. The intent of the Mini-Town Hall is to engage with your team to identify what we call *crowbar goals*, or areas where you can have the greatest impact with the least effort. Similar to the Icelandic National Assembly, it is *a replicable and scalable method* intended to engage teams in both the design and deployment of change, creating heightened levels of accountability and ownership.

The Mini-Town Hall is an interactive, action-learning process that allows the Integrator Leader to set the compass heading by defining WHAT the team focuses on while engaging critical stakeholders in HOW the change takes place. This process gets everyone into the canopy, where they can see their activities in the context of the whole operation.

The Mini-Town Hall is excellent for bringing diverse stakeholder teams together to solve problems and operationalize the mission. It is an opportunity for Integrator Leaders to listen to their team about what's working and what's not, while engaging the team in creating the solutions to the challenges they face.

Aligning Your Team for Outcome-Based Performance

As an Integrator Leader, you set the priorities (WHAT) and the rationale (WHY) to launch the Mini-Town Hall and use our process to help your team create the roadmap for HOW to get from here to there. The process itself is an extremely effective mentoring tool: you will gain uncanny insight into how individuals and whole teams are thinking and how they see your organization. This allows you to understand precisely where your guidance and intervention is needed, which you implement on a just-enough, just-in-time basis. Your intent is always to help the team stand on its own, requiring less direction from you over time.

The term *Mini* as it refers to the Mini-Town Hall does not refer to the overall size of the group, but rather to the highly interactive small group discussions that are core to this process. The process allows all participants to have the chance to engage and provide input during the meeting. The number of participants who can engage, especially when combined with virtual collaboration tools, appears limitless.

As we saw in the nation of Iceland, this approach was first used with 1,200 participants in one convention center and thousands more participating outside this main event in smaller community groups. The Mini-Town Hall process evolved through its use by hundreds of leaders in large and small organizations who routinely provide us with feedback that we have in turn used to refine the overall approach.

Setting the Stage

The setting you choose for your Mini-Town Hall should allow your team to meet free of distractions and in a place where they feel comfortable engaging in intense thought and conversation. To begin the session, you'll want to have the entire group together in the same room but, depending on the size of the group and the purpose of the Mini-Town Hall, you will break out into smaller working groups before reconvening back together. The approach we will explore next assumes your entire team is co-located together. In Chapter 10, we will discuss how to conduct this in a slightly modified process virtually for use with geographically distributed teams.

Consider keeping things a bit more informal by conducting your Mini-Town Hall over lunch or include refreshments. Give attendees advanced notice and ask that they come ready to engage and participate actively in the discussion. Be sure to set the ground rules in advance. Let them know that this is not a complaint session. Rather, it is their opportunity to engage as a team and provide you with specific suggestions as to how the operation can be improved, and what they need from you as a Leader to be successful. Let the team know you expect them to be forward-looking and constructive, and to bring alternatives and suggestions, not just problems.

Mini-Town Hall Scan and Focus Versions

In designing the Mini-Town Hall, we intentionally developed two versions: the *Scan* and the *Focus*. The Scan is used to evaluate the current state of your operation, while the Focus is used to work on specific operational challenges or strategic priorities. We recommend you periodically use the Mini-Town Hall Scan process as part of an essential FEEDBACK LOOP to engage with your team and maintain the health of your organization over time. The Focus strategy is typically used to launch a new initiative, improve a process, develop a new product or service, or generally to create new organization capacity where it did not exist before. In Chapter 11, we will explore how to create Action Teams to focus on special initiatives that emerge from this process.

Mini-Town Hall Scan

o   Provide a Canopy view of the operation

o   What is working? What is not working?

o   Identify crowbar goals for maximum impact

Mini-Town Hall Focus

o   Dive deep into specific challenges or initiatives

o   Targeted change methodology; Action Teams

o   Focus on the design and implementation of a change initiative

Moving Teams from Compliance to Commitment

Aiden was a senior leader at one of the world's largest wholesale distribution centers, a 24/7 global operation whose mission was to extend the operational reach of their customers. Aiden was hired to help his company cope with the largest surge in demand they had ever experienced in their history.

The organization was not handling the surge well. Backorders, operational errors, and customer complaints were mounting by the day. Meanwhile, many of Aiden's managers continued to approach their new reality with the *we've always done it that way* mindset. No matter how hard he pushed them to improve their metrics, the operation as a whole was failing to meet customer expectations. Aiden knew that if they were unable to keep up with escalating demand, their customers would leave and find another way to do business.

As we have seen many times, most of the individual functional groups in Aiden's operation were meeting or even exceeding their individual metrics, yet they were failing to accomplish their core mission objective of getting the right product to the right place at the right time. While their internal metrics indicated that they were meeting their target, their customers were clearly saying otherwise. This is an all-too-common example of organizational inputs not aligning with customer outcomes.

Bruce and Jim met with Aiden and spent time listening to his managers and employees, a sampling of suppliers, and some key customers. We learned that people were usually doing their job right, but not necessarily doing the right job. They were following standard operating procedures that were out-of-date. We saw minimal cross-functional coordination, as managers from one group rarely collaborated with managers of another group to solve problems. There was a lack of communication between shifts, and we rarely found anyone proactively engaging with suppliers or customers to keep them informed on a regular basis. In fact, such contact was usually initiated by the customer after a mistake or problem had already occurred.

Managers often reacted by becoming defensive, looking to place blame elsewhere. This set the tone for their employees, who blamed one another for mistakes at the operational level. Rarely did we find anyone interested in working together to determine the root cause of a problem. In fact, we frequently found that the same mistakes or problems kept reoccurring; all of which seemed to stem from failure to communicate, assuming problems were outside one's area of responsibility, a lack of current documentation and training, and little understanding of the vital role each individual and functional group played in meeting customer expectations.

Aiden asked us to assist him in conducting a Mini-Town Hall Scan to help him and his team identify what was working well and the areas that needed to be improved in their operation.

We then helped Aiden identify the critical stakeholders that needed to participate in this initial meeting. Clearly, it is often impractical to assemble all the hundreds of people from an entire operation, as large as this one, together at one time. The nature of the challenge and who is impacted by it determines who participates in the session. Ideally, you want a microcosm, or representative cross-section, of the stakeholder group participating in the meeting. The idea is to assemble a group that represents the various parties affected by the problem being addressed.

In Aiden's case, we suspected that most of their problems were cross-functional in nature, so we assembled a cross-section of approximately 70 individuals. The group included top leaders of the organization and their managers, many top performers from across the organization regardless of their rank, and nonsupervisory people from Transportation, Receiving, Storage, Distribution, Inventory, Demand Planning, Training, IT, Administration, and Client Relations. Each were assigned to worktables ensuring that there was a cross-functional mix at each table. Everyone was free to mix among other tables as needed after the initial discussion was underway.

Aiden's boss kicked off the meeting by giving a strategic perspective from the canopy. He talked about their mission, the challenges coming their way, and current performance metrics. He then brought up numerous examples of where they were clearly missing the mark from the customer's perspective. He acknowledged that, while many areas of the operation had improved, the various functional groups were not working as a team to consistently move the ball down the field and through the end zone to get the customer what they needed. He gave them the challenge of identifying the areas of the operation that needed to be improved in order to more consistently satisfy the customer.

With these challenges and priorities in mind, each group was asked to begin by discussing the following questions:

- What is working well?

- What is not working well?

- What should we do differently moving forward?

- What do we need from one another?

By midafternoon, the discussion at the tables had become so compelling that even when it was time for a break, the participants remained engaged. They were also beginning to reach out to other tables in the room to share ideas and seek information.

With their newly expanded canopy view, they quickly discovered for themselves that operations were fragmented and functioning too much in silos without complete information. Listening to the table discussions, it was evident that people were beginning to understand that the true nature of the problem was not so much *within* the functional groups, but *between* them in the white spaces of the organization chart. This turned the discussion to what each needed from one another, acknowledging that by working together they all could more effectively achieve their customers' expectations.

Each person in the room, informally representing their part of the operation, was beginning to see how they each owned a piece of the problem. One specific example: They realized the way trucks were loaded by vendors prior to reaching their distribution facility had a profound impact on how material moved through the entire system. There were multiple opportunities for errors to occur within the current loading process. Much like everything else in the operation, this impacted each person in the room and the bottom line. They were all realizing how flaws in operational processes impacted budgets, employee salaries and bonuses, and customer satisfaction.

Aiden followed up by holding several Focus versions of the Mini-Town Hall to address the specific areas of the operation identified in our original Scan meeting. Each time, they identified and included appropriate stakeholders (such as the outside vendors responsible for loading the trucks) so each could adjust their practices accordingly. Aiden soon noticed that the people reporting to him hosted their own Mini-Town Hall meetings, operating and thinking in a more cross-functional manner. He found that employees began to take more ownership of their work. This resulted in fewer errors, better metrics, improved morale, and much happier customers.

Mini-Town Hall Operational Scan

As demonstrated in the example above, using the Mini-Town Hall Scan is like shining a spotlight on all the key functions and processes of your operation. We ask what is working, what is not, what can we do differently, and what do we need from each other? Answers to these questions help to maintain a critical barometer on the vital signs of the operation, helping you sustain a high level of performance over time.

Assuming everything in a given area checks out, we move on with our Scan by moving the spotlight, as it were, to a new area. When your spotlight reveals a particular problem, challenge, or process that requires more *focused attention*, we then move to the Focus version of the Mini-Town Hall. Here we channel the team's efforts in a specific direction, at a minimum creating a tangible outcome that can be pilot tested. This keeps the team moving toward a solution without getting stuck in analysis paralysis.

If you are focusing on a specific initiative such as a new product or service launch that will require the coordinated and focused effort of the team over time, we recommend you use Action Teams, a topic we will explore in Chapter 11.

Integrator Leader Reflections

- How has the Change Integrator challenged or reaffirmed your own approach to leadership? What changes do you want to make to your own approach?

- How do you plan to use the Change Integrator to structure your Mini-Town Hall events?

- Who should participate in your Mini-Town Hall to ensure that the appropriate stakeholders are involved?

CHAPTER SIX

Setting Your Compass Heading

"People work better when they know what the goal is
and why. It's important that people look forward
to coming to work."
Elon Musk

Defining our PURPOSE begins with seeing the world from the canopy view. The idea is to widen everyone's aperture so that they see their actions within the broader organizational context.

Purpose: Defining Your Strategic Direction

PURPOSE defines WHAT we are here to accomplish, and as such, it serves as your compass heading or your strategic direction. It needs to be clear, concise, and compelling. Your PURPOSE consists of three fundamental components that we will explore in this section:

1. Strategic Priorities

2. Outcome-Based Success Criteria

3. Expectations of Performance Linked to Priorities

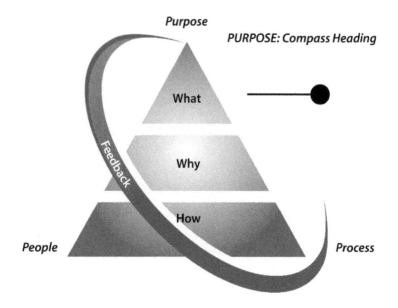

Begin by outlining your organization's PURPOSE or strategic intent. This should include any key strategic priorities or special initiatives coming your way. Do not make the mistake of assuming everyone understands the common PURPOSE. Knowledge workers are inherently myopic; that is, they possess a deep, yet fragmented, knowledge. Without a clear compass heading to orient their activities, knowledge workers will never be fully productive.

Providing your team with a view from the canopy gives them a clear line of sight to their goal. Show them where they are going and then ask them HOW to get there. Mentor, coach, and guide—but don't tell them HOW. Help them learn to self-organize behind your intent and become less dependent upon you over time.

Advancing by Working Yourself Out of Your Job

Frustrated with his team, overworked and burned out, Brandon was seriously considering quitting his job managing a large warehouse complex and acres of outdoor storage. The job was tough, and at times downright gritty. He had been brought in to help prepare for a major expansion of the operation and was rewriting standard operating procedures using a new enterprise resource planning (ERP) management system. His crew was in disarray, many were new, some were so frustrated they were looking for another job, and others were just doing enough to get by until they retired.

While Brandon made significant progress in reducing errors and cleaning up aging inventory, trying to push his team harder didn't work. Instead, his hard-driving style resulted in union grievances filed against him. Brandon had plenty of experience managing large operations, but this style of leading did not get him far. Try as he might, he could not turn this operation around. The morale of the team was declining, and their performance was suffering.

Brandon participated in one-on-one leadership coaching provided by our company. This involved taking part in a 360 multi-source survey where he received feedback from his superiors, peers, direct reports, and others on his performance. Brandon received high marks for his analytical, organizational and problem-solving skills, his ability to multitask, and his incredible drive to get things done. On the other hand, he received low scores on listening to others, involving them in the planning process, and delegating to his team. Further, his drive to get things done was often perceived by others as being rigid and dictatorial.

His team instead wanted Brandon to *ask them how* they would deal with problems as they arise, rather than telling them how to fix them. They wanted to share their insights. They wanted Brandon to listen to them first about what changes needed to be made, discuss them as a team, and then implement the suggestions.

As his coach, Bruce's first advice to Brandon was "rather than quit your job, work yourself out of your job." As he was burnt out, this got Brandon's attention. After some explanation, he admitted that he had never seriously engaged with his team to gain their input on HOW to improve the operation. The coming surge would be the perfect opportunity to do so.

Bruce suggested to Brandon that he conduct a Mini-Town Hall Scan with his team, giving them a view from the canopy about the surge coming their way, and get them involved in HOW to handle it. Ask, rather than tell them HOW to accomplish their mission, and use the whole process as a developmental opportunity. Mentor and coach them, but don't tell them HOW. The more you help them to self-organize behind your intent, the less dependent upon you they will become. "After all," Bruce asked, "what do you have to lose?"

While clearly a bit skeptical, Brandon conducted his first of what would become a series of Mini-Town Hall meetings with his team. To give his team the view from the canopy, he took a barbecue out to the edge of the warehouse complex overlooking the huge outdoor area that would soon have to be organized to accommodate the coming surge of material. While enjoying lunch, Brandon asked his team to imagine their new operation up and running. He said, "Collectively, you all know this place better than I do and now you know your mission. The question is, how do you want to move forward? What is working and what is not in our current operation, and what would you do differently to accommodate our coming surge? Give it your best shot, I'm all ears."

He then asked them to talk in small groups and brainstorm their ideas. To his amazement, they came up with a basic structure and workflow for the new operation during this first meeting and refined their approach in a series of subsequent informal planning sessions. They also told Brandon that they wanted more training to prepare, but not the standard training they usually received. Instead, they came up with a list of topics to train on that were important to the operation, then they matched these topics to team members with those skills who could lead the training events.

His team was soon confident that they had a strategy for moving forward. After listening carefully, asking clarifying questions, and ensuring they had their bases covered, Brandon gave them the go-ahead to execute their plan. Later he would confide to Bruce that his team's plan was better than his—and because they owned it, they wouldn't let it fail.

Before they had a chance to fully implement their plan, Brandon went on two weeks of vacation, during which time he became ill and was out of work for nearly a month. He said he found himself lying in bed not only feeling physically ill, but increasingly anxious and dreading the thought of going back to work.

His first morning back, Brandon did not recognize his own operation. Much of the surge had already arrived, and had been sorted, categorized, and stored across the vastly expanded complex. Much of this was accomplished with the plan developed and executed by his team while he had been gone. As he walked around reacquainting himself with his own operation, one of his employees, who rarely ever spoke up in the past, spotted Brandon, and with a beaming grin said, "Welcome back boss! Are you lost? Do you need a map back to your office? We have everything under control here."

Amazed and a bit bewildered, once back in his office, Brandon soon noticed there was no one running to him with brushfires to put out. His operation was humming along better than ever before. After several months, his team had improved their performance to achieve 98% inventory accuracy, while cutting their backlog in half. In turn, he went out of his way to ensure that they received recognition for their extraordinary efforts and the outcomes they achieved, resulting in several team members receiving awards and promotions.

Brandon not only stopped planning to quit, he got a major promotion to Regional Director where he used the same approach to help turn around several operations within his expanded territory. After a second 360 multi-source feedback survey, Brandon received the highest marks across the board. His staff wrote at length how they appreciated his listening skills, how they were included in decisions that affected their work, and Brandon's recognition of their efforts. Brandon's boss was clearly pleased with the superior results and dramatically improved morale, resulting in less absenteeism and fewer complaints.

Brandon later told Bruce that his marriage improved because he practiced these same principles at home with his family. Although his span of responsibility greatly increased, Brandon said his stress level went down and that for the first time in his adult life he could go on vacation and not worry about his operation. His team assured him, "We have everything under control…"

Brandon's story is not unique—instead it is something we have witnessed many times with our clients. Often the fastest route to advancement is to work yourself out of your job. This is done by building an ownership mentality in your team.

Asking Your Team What They Would Change

This is the question Joyce, a leader of an IT organization within a large aerospace enterprise, used to open her Mini-Town Hall Scan: "If you were in charge, what would you change?" This got her team's attention but did require a bit more explanation.

Joyce challenged everyone to look at their job in new ways, to simplify, streamline, and find ways to make their job easier while achieving the intended outcome. She encouraged them to stretch and learn other skills beyond those in their current role. This meant not only learning a new skill but being willing to teach each other as well. She told them why a versatile employee is a valuable employee and how this mindset would make the whole organization smarter, make their jobs easier, and position them for potential advancement.

The team was quiet at first, intrigued but apparently not sure exactly where to begin. This is not uncommon. The mistake many leaders make at this point is to jump in to fill the void too soon, turning the attention of the group back on the leader. This defeats the purpose, because the point is to make our teams *less dependent on us* moving forward. Eventually, one person spoke up, then another, and soon a lively discussion ensued. Once focused conversations were well underway, Joyce left the room and told them she would be back to reengage with them about the ideas that emerged.

Joyce returned to the room to witness a very lively discussion.

The team had produced a draft plan to streamline their key processes, a job rotation schedule, and a cross-training regimen so that everyone could perform the duties in their new rotational assignments. At the team's request, they met several more times to work out the details on their plan before putting it into action.

In her feedback to Bruce, Joyce wrote: "From this suggestion, we agreed to establish a quarterly rotation schedule for the different kinds of workloads we have, essentially allowing our section to specialize on a specific type of work for that quarter. Next quarter they get a different type of workload and so on."[21]

After implementing this new process for several months, Joyce pulled her team's production reports for a specified period and compared them to an equivalent period after implementation of this new practice. She wrote, "The results speak for themselves: our across-the-board average production rose by 30.79% with some types of workload exceeding 50%, one was 60.71%. An amazing step in the right direction!"

Positive changes in morale also became evident. The team was more engaged, and they found a new sense of camaraderie as they began training one another, learning new skills, and receiving recognition for their improved performance. Those subject matter experts (SME Trainers) who conducted the training received additional recognition for updating the standard operating procedures for their area and for training their colleagues. The new procedures were then uploaded on a shared drive and made into desktop guides bearing the names of the SME Trainers who created them.

Most importantly, they were not doing this because they were told to by their boss, but instead they saw the benefit for themselves and took ownership of the initiative. They were learning to see their own work in relation to the operation differently, and their behavior changed accordingly.

Most of Joyce's team had been together for years, doing their work much the same way they always had. But they were dutifully following processes rather than evaluating and improving them. What had changed in the team after experiencing the Mini-Town Hall is that, *rather than simply taking orders, they were taking ownership.*

How to Build an Ownership Mentality in Your Team

To build an ownership mentality in your team, begin by outlining WHAT challenges and changes are coming, WHY they are important, and HOW they will impact your team. Summarize the mission of your organization, your key strategic priorities, and your expectations of performance. Tie your expectations of performance to the outcomes you expect your team to create. Everyone on your team must understand that you will hold them accountable for these outcomes and not just inputs.

When defining your PURPOSE, focus on the following three key categories:

1. Strategic Priorities: WHAT are your core priorities? This should flow from your organization's strategic guidance to the priorities of your division or branch. Paint a picture for your team so that they can see their own desired end state based on what the customer expects in the form of an integrated solution to their problem.

2. Outcome-Based Success Criteria: WHAT *are the criteria by*

which you will determine a successful outcome? On what criteria will your end-user or customer judge a successful outcome? WHAT are the gaps between what your customer expects and what you are delivering? WHAT are the key milestones along the way that you expect your team to achieve, and by when?

3. Expectations of Performance (Linked to Priorities): It is important that you tie individual and team performance ratings to the outcomes you expect them to produce. Activity does not equal progress. We have often witnessed large organizations whose major functional groups were meeting or exceeding their performance metrics, but the goods and services the organization produced were below par. Customers expect integrated solutions to their problems, and integrated solutions require integrated operations. This means that workers need to self-organize and integrate cross-functionally to achieve the results customers expect.

Steve Jobs believed that people didn't know they needed an Apple product until they used one. This is because Jobs and his team intentionally designed Apple products to create integrated, user-friendly solutions to customer wants and needs.

They did not wait for the customer to tell them what they wanted. The most innovative firms today anticipate customer needs based on a methodical form of empathic observation and questioning, where they place themselves in the customer's shoes and look out at their world through their eyes. How can you do the same for your customer, whether internal or external to your organization, to create integrated solutions to their problems?

Why: The Rationale for Change

Before you proceed to small group discussions, your team must understand the rationale for any changes or new priorities that either you propose or that emerge from the group's discussion within the following three key categories:

1. WHY will this change benefit our customer?

2. WHY will this change benefit our organization?

3. WHY will this change benefit individuals?

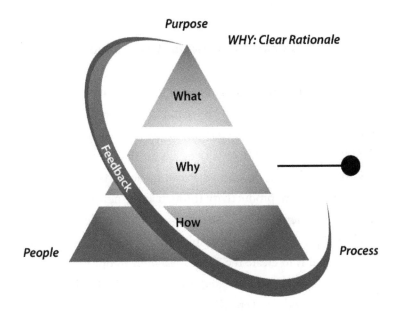

Why Will This Change Benefit Our Customer?

Any change you or the team proposes must first clearly make life better for your customer. Looking back at the Change Integrator, the top of the triangle represents the PURPOSE of your organization, and this must always be focused on the outcomes achieved for your customer. It is always best to assume that your customer does not want what you are selling. Instead, what customers want are integrated solutions to their problems. Therefore, any change proposed must first be focused on this PURPOSE, which is the main reason for the existence of your organization. Be succinct; you (or any team member who proposes a change) must first ask WHY the change you are proposing will make life better for your customer.

Why Will This Change Benefit Our Organization?

Our goal as Integrator Leaders is not only to make our organization more effective and efficient, but a better place to work. The more enlightened leaders we work with understand that they should improve the quality of life for their employees. This pays dividends well beyond what can be achieved by trying to squeeze out more productivity through some new management fad or efficiency measure. Integrator Leaders understand that happy people *are* productive employees.

Our goal is to create the *owner's mentality* in our workers. We want people to have a stake and a sense of ownership in the outcomes they produce. Peter Drucker encouraged leaders to treat knowledge workers as volunteers, and as such you must engage your team and elicit the very best they have to offer your organization. Do this by creating a work environment that is both meaningful and rewarding for them. This approach will also help you attract, develop, and retain top talent.

Why Will This Change Benefit Individuals?

Knowledge workers tend to be more committed to the development of their own portfolio of skills than they are to any organization. Most often, these people don't quit the company—they quit their boss. And this doesn't necessarily mean that the boss is a jerk; it means that individuals simply may not feel important to the organization in a meaningful way. Knowledge workers want to be part of the changes that affect them. They want a place where they can learn, grow, and develop their skills. They want equal measures of autonomy and teamwork where they can sharpen one another's skills, share best practices, and collaborate on projects.

Many of today's employees watched their parents devote themselves selflessly, often for decades, to their employers, only to be treated like pawns in a chess game. They experienced relentless waves of automation, downsizing, offshoring, and other short-sighted corporate strategies where workers were viewed as costs to be reduced or eliminated altogether. This taught new generations of workers that they needed to watch out for themselves. The best leaders we work with understand that people want to be part of an organization where they continually learn, develop their skills, are rewarded for their contributions, and in short, become more marketable.

What's in It for Me?

Another way of looking at the question above is to ask your team members, "What's in it for you to actively engage in this change process?" Remind them that their path to future advancement lies in improving the current operation.

Conversely, remind your team that *change is either done with them or to them.* That is, in the end, we all have two choices: we can either continuously grow, learn, and innovate, or run the risk of having change forced upon us by an external competitor or the meddling of upper management. Let them know that, to the extent they take this Mini-Town Hall process seriously, you will take their ideas seriously.

Integrator Leader Reflections

- What are your three top strategic priorities, and the outcomes-based criteria for achieving them?

- Why will achieving these priorities benefit your customer, your organization, and your team members?

- How will you link your expectations of performance to the outcomes you want your team to achieve?

CHAPTER SEVEN

Engaging Your Team

"People want to feel what they do makes a difference."
Frances Hesselbein

Now that you have defined your compass heading, it is time to ask your team to create the roadmap to get you there. *Ask, don't tell*; coach, mentor, and guide them, but don't tell them HOW. Never allow process to be a substitute for thinking. Tell your team that you don't want them to simply follow processes; but instead you expect them to analyze and perfect them.

How: Crafting the Roadmap

SpaceX and Tesla Motors Founder Elon Musk feels passionate about his team being creative and innovative thinkers. Musk goes so far as to say, "I don't believe in process. In fact, when I interview a potential employee and he or she says that 'it's all about the process,' I see that as a bad sign."[22]

Clearly, Musk is not advocating a complete absence of process. Instead, we do not want our standard operating procedures to become substitutes for thinking and straitjackets that limit our ability to think and act creatively. We need to stay out of the *prison of the known* by continually looking for new and better ways to meet our mission. Rather than focusing on following a process, the focus must be on the outcome we achieve.

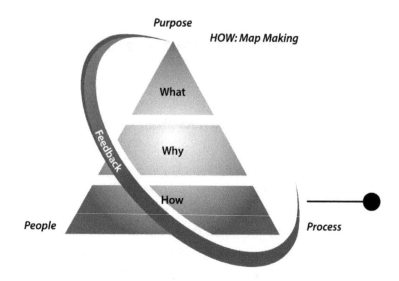

Your team may not always come up with the best solution the first time, though with practice they will often amaze you. However, by asking first and then listening carefully to their responses, you will know exactly how they are thinking. This window into your team's psyche is invaluable as it allows you to calibrate your coaching accordingly. Your goal is to guide your team to their own solution. The more they own the solution, the less you will have to manage them, and the happier your customers will be.

Who's on The Bus?

When we refer to the PEOPLE quadrant of the Change Integrator, this refers to a broad group of stakeholders both within and outside of your organization who will be affected by the change. To the extent they will be affected by it, we want to include them in how we design and implement the change.

Once you are clear about your PURPOSE (or strategic intent), you must ask yourself who is on the bus,[23] in what seats, with what competencies? That is, before you go further, you must make sure you have the right team, and more broadly speaking the right set of stakeholders at the table. The team members you choose must be both *willing and able* to perform the mission. If they lack either the willingness or the ability, they may be disqualified.

Who Would You Rehire?

The quickest way to gain a barometer on the quality and capability of your team is to ask yourself: "Who would I rehire tomorrow?" Take out a sheet of paper; at the top, write down your core mission priorities and the core competencies necessary to perform this mission. Below that, make three columns, one titled *name*, the second titled *rehire / don't rehire*, and the third titled *why or why not*.

Starting with the leadership in your organization and then working through the operational ranks, write down everyone's name in column one; note either *rehire* or *don't rehire* beside the name in column two; in column three, make a brief note why you would or would not rehire them.

Now look at those you indicated as *don't rehire* and the reason why you would not rehire them. Ask yourself: "Is the reason that I would not rehire this person *due to their willingness or their ability* to perform their duties in support of our mission?" If it is a question of ability, you can often remedy this through appropriate training and development or finding a more suitable role for them. If, however, you would not rehire the person due to their willingness or attitude, then you have a more difficult problem on your hands, and one that you may not be able to easily change.

If individuals on your team are struggling because of their willingness or attitude toward their work or toward their teammates, you must have a direct conversation with these individuals about their attitude and the impact this is having on the organization.

Further, if the person with the attitude problem is in leadership, it is of the utmost importance that this issue be addressed promptly. Anyone in a leadership position must be held to a higher standard due to the greater level of influence and impact they have on those around them and those who report to them. Leaders set the tone for their teams; you must have the right people in leadership positions who are fully on board with the direction the organization is moving.

Your time and energy should be focused on those who demonstrate themselves both willing and able to become an integral part of the team and mission. Too often, we spend a disproportionate amount of time on a handful of people who simply may not be a good fit. When this occurs, we must act in the best interests of our organization and mission by assisting these individuals either into a more suitable seat or off the bus altogether.

Assuming you would *rehire* the person, we recommend that

you routinely do so. That is, rehire your best people on a routine basis. What do we mean by this? Too often it is only during the hiring phase, when we are "courting" these individuals, that we share our vision of the organization with them and do our best to entice them to join us on the journey ahead. We make promises of a bright future and all the good things that will come their way if they join the organization.

Over time, the shine and promise of a great future full of rewards and recognition may begin to fade. We've all heard the saying that we join an organization for many different reasons, but we often leave because of a bad boss. And what makes a bad boss? A bad boss may simply be one who fails to provide opportunities for employees to learn and develop new skills or provide timely and actionable feedback on their performance.

Most employees spend more waking hours at work than at home, so it is important to make our workplace somewhere that people want to come to learn, grow, develop healthy relationships, and build their future. If we fail to create a culture that attracts, develops, and retains top talent, our best people will be the first ones to leave.

The lesson here is, always rehire your best people, keep them engaged, show genuine interest in their future goals and their passions. Provide avenues for them to grow and develop their skills. Mentor and coach them in a way that you would want to be mentored and coached yourself. Help them to align their passions and interests with the direction the organization is moving. Tie rewards and recognition to this and ensure that their goals remain aligned with those of the organization. This creates a win for your organization, for your personnel, and for your customers.

Next, we will explore how to create self-organizing teams capable of creating the integrated solutions your customers expect.

See the World Through Your Customer's Eyes

Isaac, a seasoned manager with a solid information technology background, was hired to create a team in the Florida panhandle area for a new client. His company had just won a multi-year contract to provide IT support services to a newly established Department of Defense training facility staffed with a large military and civilian workforce spread over three geographically dispersed areas. Isaac would be leading an experienced group of technicians, but few of them had ever worked together before.

Isaac needed to rapidly assemble his team, organize, and hit the ground running to ensure the training staff could begin their work within 90 days. Though there were plenty of challenges to work through, generally things seemed to be manageable until Isaac was told that a separate IT support building had not been allocated for them. Instead, his IT support team would be housed in a building that was already occupied by the training operations and assessment team. To add to this bad news, the small, cramped area that would be their new home was in the back portion of a building without any direct exterior access. All of Isaac's team would have to walk through the other work sections to enter or exit the building, something they would constantly be doing throughout the day as they responded to numerous setup requests and trouble tickets on the base.

Isaac was concerned that the current tenants of the building would soon become irritated by the constant movement in and out of the building as well as the increased noise levels in their work space. As Isaac assessed the situation, he figured he had two choices: either fail, which was not an option, or look at the challenge as an opportunity.

As his coach, Jim advised Isaac to use the Mini-Town Hall Scan to engage his newly formed team about their mission, provide them his compass heading and priorities, and then let the team discuss how best to address the challenges that lay ahead. After some follow-up coaching with Jim, Isaac felt ready to give it a try.

Since he enjoyed grilling, it was natural for Isaac to use lunchtime to conduct the Mini-Town Hall meetings. He volunteered to bring the grill and asked the team to organize the rest. While his team worked out all the details for lunch, grilling, and cleanup, Isaac prepared to share his vision for the organization and how their work supported the objectives at headquarters. He also arranged to have his team briefed on the mission of the base and how their team supported the training of the Airmen stationed there.

While having lunch with his team, Isaac began describing their mission, and why it was vital to the overall training mission of the base. "Without a fully operational IT capability," he told them, "the classroom, simulator, and exercise training programs could not be conducted". He encouraged them to see the operation through their customers' eyes, anticipate what they need, and integrate seamlessly into their operation.

He gave them a clear picture of the outcome the customer expected them to achieve, broken down into key objectives for both the Setup and Sustainment Phases of the operation. He then outlined a number of challenges he foresaw that he wanted them to discuss as a team. He underscored his expectation that everyone would work together based on three guiding principles: 1) always WE, not ME; 2) see the world through your customers' eyes; 3) think and act cross-functionally.

Once he was sure everyone was clear about their new compass heading, Isaac asked them to create the plan to execute the Setup Phase of the operation. He then politely excused himself, telling the team he'd return by midafternoon. A bit bewildered, the team asked where he was going, as they assumed he would lead the planning discussion. Isaac just smiled and assured them that they were all experienced professionals, and if the plan they developed was as good as today's lunch, the customer would be very pleased.

Preparing the lunch proved to be a good team-building exercise. By the time he joined them for another meal a few days later, the team was already on a first-name basis. Observing their interactions, Isaac began to see informal leaders rising naturally within his team. He also noticed that the incumbent tenants were growing increasingly curious about what was taking place just outside "their building."

Isaac shared with Jim during a follow up coaching session that the Friday lunchtime Mini-Town Halls became standard practice for his team. He went on to say that he was ecstatic when he found out that without his direction, his team began to invite others to attend the Mini-Town Halls, including their customers from the training detachments, base support operations, higher headquarters, and the tenants of the building they now shared. This informal approach to building cross-functional relationships opened doors and broke down barriers. It also created a path for Isaac's team to learn about the operation through their customer's eyes, identifying potential problems before they arose, and making their customers very pleased in the process.

Soon after this, he was notified by base operations that they had found an ideal new space for Isaac's IT support team in a building centrally located among all the customers that his team supported. The facilities had appropriate security, power sources, cooling for servers, a training room and work room, and easy access for support technicians and walk-in customers—and of course, space for a barbecue.

Isaac's team completed the Setup Phase ahead of schedule and, because they had been proactive in developing a plan for the Sustainment Phase, the customer was able to begin their training operations early. Isaac and his team had built critical cross-functional relationships through their Friday Mini-Town Hall lunches and quickly became the *go-to team* on base for IT issues.

Even outside of work on their own time, the team became committed to the "WE VS. ME" philosophy. When a young member of the team was diagnosed with cancer, his teammates jumped in to help. While he recovered from chemotherapy, his teammates donated their unused vacation time to him, maintained his house and lawn, and kept in contact with his wife, often dropping by his house with a home-cooked dinner.

Over the course of the four-year contract, five technicians were hired into permanent government jobs, representing significant career advancement. Each subsequent option year of the contract was fully funded, and the team received top ratings on each of their annual contractor performance assessments.

By *seeing the operation through their customer's* eyes, Isaac defined his compass heading and rationale (WHAT and WHY), and then allowed his team maximum latitude to come up with the roadmap for HOW to operationalize their mission. The Mini-Town Hall process fostered a sense of camaraderie and ownership in his team, helped them forge vital relationships with their customers and key stakeholders, and served as a vital FEEDBACK LOOP throughout the process.

The Feedback Loop

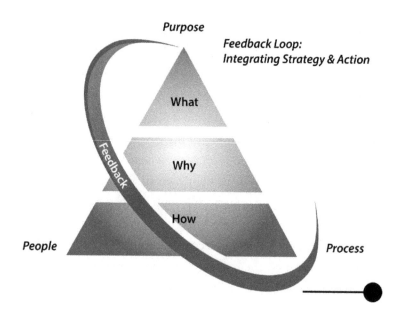

We have frequently seen knowledge and expertise hidden away inside people's heads, or within pockets of the organization, where it is not widely shared and therefore cannot make the rest of the system smarter. This problem can be endemic within large, complex organizations that follow rigid operational procedures and lines of authority. Too often, critical knowledge exists within silos and stovepipes, meaning that many organizations literally do not know what they know.

The FEEDBACK LOOP on the Change Integrator represents a constant real-time source of information between strategy and action, and between cross-functional groups within your organization. We need an effective FEEDBACK LOOP to ensure that everyone understands the mission and how their activities support it. The FEEDBACK LOOP also helps functional groups better understand what they need from one another.

As an Integrator Leader, you can't over-communicate; and communication requires learning to listen as well. Listen closely to your own people and utilize the critical *operational intelligence* that exists throughout the organization.

Let your team know that you are not only open to their input, but *that you expect it.* That is, you want them to analyze and improve processes, rather than simply follow them. In fact, you want them to come up with the entire plan while you mentor and guide them just enough along the way to assure that the plan becomes theirs and not yours.

Demonstrate through your actions that you are willing to incorporate appropriate input in service of the mission and give them all the credit and recognition for their ideas. Conversely, if you are unable to use their input, do your best to explain why their suggestion cannot be implemented. Assess all ideas on their merits regardless of position or grade of the one who originated the idea.

To create an environment where feedback is encouraged, you as the leader must model this behavior by routinely asking for feedback and input from your team. Conversely, you should also challenge your team's ideas, as appropriate, based on the needs of the mission.[24] It is their job to sell you on the merits of their idea by explaining WHY it will benefit the mission, and it is your job to explain why the idea cannot be implemented when that is the case.

The key is to be as transparent as possible in this process to build a foundation of trust in the team. Be patient, and do not expect that your people will always get it right the first time.

Jumpstarting Team Dialogue

Now that you have given your team a view from the canopy and a clear compass heading and rationale for change as the focus for your Mini-Town Hall, it's time to get them engaged in creating the roadmap to achieve their mission. To get the conversation started, we suggest that you divide attendees into groups of approximately five to eight each and ask that someone volunteer at each table to record the suggestions that emerge.

We suggest you give careful thought to who is sitting at each table, combining people who need to work closer together in practice so that they are grouped in a way that stimulates communication and knowledge sharing. Ask that participants write their own answers down first before sharing with the group. This helps ensure that people are not filtering their input or being unduly swayed by others in the group. Remind them that *consensus is not the goal,* but rather you are looking for constructive, forward-looking input while avoiding the tendency for groupthink. The key is to get everyone's input on the table before determining the course ahead.

Key Questions to Ask

While the questions you ask will change depending on the purpose of the Mini-Town Hall, a good place to start is with the Scan version. The Mini-Town Hall Scan is also an excellent exercise to perform at critical junctures during any change initiative to help keep everyone aligned and on target. To perform a Scan, start off by asking your team the following questions:

Given our PURPOSE and strategic priorities:

- What is working well?

- What is not working well?

- What should we do differently moving forward?

- What do we need from one another?

Additional questions are provided at the end of this chapter which may be helpful as your team proceeds or as you focus on specific challenges.

What Is Working Well?

The reason we ask this question is twofold: first, we want to start out on a positive note and provide some recognition for the team's successes and things they are most proud of. Second, we want to reinforce and build upon those things that are already working well. Quite frequently, top-down-driven change disrupts the very things that are working well. This may not be intentional, but if someone who is two or three levels (or two or three thousand miles) removed from the operation is designing a change, there are bound to be unintended consequences. Once again, the upper echelons rarely know as much about a job as the person doing it. So quite simply, we want to identify, reinforce, and build upon those aspects of the operation that are already functioning well.

What Is Not Working Well?

The primary ground rule here is that we all agree to be constructive and forward-looking in our remarks. We are not here to name names or throw others under the bus. Instead, ask the team to reflect upon the operation as a whole—from the canopy view, the processes now in place, the level and quality of communication within the team, and between your team and other functional departments with whom they must coordinate their activities.

We want the team to see their operation from the canopy view and objectively observe their operation. Rather than simply following processes, we are asking them to step back to observe and evaluate the processes themselves. The key is to get them off the jungle floor to see their operation from above, as an integrated whole.

Said another way, ask your team to imagine that they are a pro sports team watching the video of their own performance in yesterday's game. No matter how good the game plan is, the best teams routinely pause to critique their own performance, so they can constantly improve. As one client put it, "You don't have to be sick to get better." Ask your people to be candid and constructive; we cannot fix something if we don't identify it as a problem.

Ask that they think of the questions in terms of their own team first, then widen their aperture to think about what is not working in relation to those with whom the team must coordinate to get the ball down the field and through the end zone. Often, one part of the organization may be operating at optimal capacity, but once the ball is handed off to another part of the organization, it is dropped, held too long, or fumbled. This is because too often these other parts of the organization may be operating based on a different set of key priorities, metrics, and measures.

This misalignment is very common in highly complex organizations with many specialized functions and divisions, each containing specialized knowledge workers. The point is that if we fail to coordinate with these other parts of the organization, we cannot achieve optimal outcomes—regardless of how well we do our part. A key role of the Integrator Leader is to help the team recognize that we cannot produce integrated solutions for our customers when we are fragmented internally.

What Should We Do Differently Moving Forward?

This question asks the team to come up with proactive, constructive ideas as to what can be done differently. The Mini-Town Hall should never be used as a complaint session. Knowledge workers must define the tasks necessary to accomplish the mission. Make it very clear that you expect them to always come to the table with ideas and alternatives—not just problems. Get them to focus on what they can control and influence first. While they can raise problems that are outside their control, their time should be spent on those issues and problems within their sphere of influence. As former U.S. President Teddy Roosevelt was famous for saying, "Do what you can, with what you have, where you are."

While you may not necessarily get full-blown, detailed solutions to the problems identified in every Mini-Town Hall, when they leave this meeting they should be very clear about where they will *put their crowbar*. That is, they should understand the areas they need to focus on to create maximum leverage and impact in moving the organization forward—and take consistent action in this new direction. This is very important; often we complain about the past or the present state without thinking about what we can do moving forward.

Remember the Zen saying: *the obstacle is the path*. This is also the philosophy of most successful leaders. The secret is in how you frame the problem—help your team transform their challenges into opportunities.

What Do We Need from Each Other?

The most complex challenges we face today cannot be solved by any single individual or functional group—and this includes you as an Integrator Leader. If we want to create integrated solutions, we need to first know what we need from each other to be successful. This includes asking your team what they need from you as their leader. Let the team know that, while you will hold them accountable for the outcomes they achieve, you exist ultimately to help them succeed.

Remind your team that no one is an island unto themselves; we are all in this together. If we do not have efficient flows of information and knowledge within the team and across the critical functions of the organization, the outcome we achieve will be less than optimal, if not disastrous. If an initiative goes sideways, we do not want to provide employees or management with a convenient excuse to say, "It's not our fault, we did our job." To eliminate this problem and any ex-post-facto excuses about why things didn't work, we must build effective channels of cross-functional communication, coordination, and integration into our change effort up front.

What we are speaking of here is fundamental to the concept of knowledge management and knowledge transfer. While information systems are one important aspect of knowledge management, they are not synonymous with it. That is, good knowledge management systems should be as transparent and user-friendly as possible in facilitating the flow of critical information required to coordinate tasks across functions within the enterprise.

Peter Drucker believed that knowledge management is fundamentally about everyone within the organization asking two basic questions: [25]

1. What do I need from you, in what form, and by when?

2. What do you need from me, by when, and in what form?

Asked another way, *seeing the operation through the eyes of our peers*, what do we need from each other to successfully fulfill our mission? Cross-training within a team and between interdependent departments and divisions goes a long way toward furthering this objective. Walking a mile in another's shoes is still one of our best antidotes to organizational misalignment. This creates a form of organizational empathy that helps us focus on shared goals and objectives. Quite simply, we need to see the big picture and what the end zone looks like, then zoom out and ask ourselves what we need from each other to move the ball down the field, through the end zone, and to replicate this process in a flexible and nimble fashion moving forward.

Other Questions to Consider

The questions that we use to guide the Mini-Town Hall discussion will of course change based on the needs of the situation, and whether you are doing a Scan or Focus version. Therefore, consider asking some of the following questions as part of your team dialogue or during follow-on sessions as appropriate:

1. Seeing the world through our customers' eyes, how can we better anticipate their needs?

2. Does this situation require refining existing processes or generating new ones?

3. Knowing what we know today, how should we organize ourselves to accomplish our mission?

4. If you had a magic wand, what are the three things you would do to improve our operation?

5. Seeing through the eyes of our peers, what do we need from other functional areas in the organization to be successful and how can we include them in this process?

6. What resources do we need to accomplish our objectives and why?

7. What barriers do we foresee and how can we overcome them?

8. What do you need from me as your leader?

Integrator Leader Reflections

- Do you have an effective FEEDBACK LOOP operating in your organization? Do you know what you know?

- Are you actively engaging your team in creating the roadmap to accomplish the mission?

- Does your team understand what they need from one another to succeed in their mission?

CHAPTER EIGHT

Creating Self-Organizing Teams

"Listen, learn ... then lead."

Stanley A. McChrystal
General, U.S. Army, Retired

We must challenge the implicit assumption that the leader should be the smartest person in the room, and that subordinates are there to receive direction and then carry out their orders. The problem is that too often people will be overly deferential to those in authority, carefully calibrating their words based on how they think a person with power may react. This constrains innovation and creativity in your team and may mean that you are missing valuable operational intelligence when you make decisions.

Leaders Leave the Room

Just as Isaac did in the previous chapter, the way to solve this problem is to simply leave the room. That is, once your team is clear about your compass heading and priorities for the Mini-Town Hall, we suggest that you and any other leaders step back to give the team space to talk openly amongst themselves.

Tell them when you'll be back to check on their progress. Make sure that they have appropriate resources such as flip charts, markers, and anything else that will help them brainstorm and capture their thoughts.

Ask for one volunteer at each table to take notes of any outcomes or decisions for the group. Participants may choose to rotate among tables as the discussion progresses, but the note-taker should stay at their original table so they can collect input from everyone who rotates through.

Leaders Return to the Room

After your team has had the chance to speak openly, return to the room to see how they are doing. Ask them if they are ready to share their thoughts or if they need more time to wrap up. When you step into the room, pay close attention to body language and the tone of the discussion. Who appears engaged, and who is sitting back with their arms folded? Are they being argumentative or are they listening to one another and building off each other's ideas? Ask each group what they came up with and capture their thinking in front of the room for everyone to see.

Seeing the Operations Through the Eyes of Your Team

Your first goal is to be sure that you understand what they are saying from their point of view. Ask questions like, "If I understand you correctly…" or "This is what I hear you saying…" or "…Is that correct?" You should also ask them to demonstrate WHY they think certain actions or changes are required, and WHY these ideas will benefit your customers and your operation.

Be sure to listen for what is not being said. Are they missing critical details? Are they thinking too narrowly from their own functional perspective? Are they missing the big picture? Who else should be in the meeting that might be affected by the problem at hand? Effective listening and questioning are critical traits of an Integrator Leader. Once everyone feels comfortable that you have listened fully and understood their ideas, it is time to think out loud with your team.

Thinking Out Loud with Your Team

Make a habit of thinking out loud with your team. Rather than giving them answers, help them follow your train of thought to arrive at an appropriate solution. Most importantly, expose them to your source code—*the values, rationale, and ethical standards* that underlie your decision-making process. At the end of the day, it does them no good for you to give them answers. Instead, you want them to own the decisions—anticipate what a situation requires, think for themselves, and work as a team to self-organize around a solution. This helps them to become less dependent upon you over time.

Once your team understands your WHAT and WHY, asking them HOW allows you to have a window into their consciousness and their way of seeing the operation. Now as a leader, you know exactly how your team is thinking, and you can adjust your mentoring accordingly. The key is to ultimately help them think on their own and self-organize behind your intent.

Three Step Problem-Solving Process

Tell your team that when they encounter a challenge, you expect them to follow these three basic steps:

1. Research the problem yourself

2. Learn from each other

3. Come to me with ideas, not just problems

If a person is unable to solve their problem through Step 1, you know you have a knowledge management or process documentation issue that needs to be addressed. Step 2 asks them to learn from each other, which promotes teamwork, networking, and knowledge sharing. Once they have taken the first two steps themselves, ask them to come to you with their best ideas and then *think out loud* with them. Help them think through their own problem, ultimately owning the solution while learning from the process of getting there.

Next, we will see how, when faced with a shortage of highly skilled personnel, one team self-organized to create an *Internal Development Path* where team members routinely hone one another's skills. This has proven to be a highly engaging and effective practice that is spreading quickly among many of our clients. They find an Internal Development Path to be a powerful complement to formal training.

The Internal Development Path

Mary is a Strategic Acquisitions Specialist for a network of high-technology manufacturing facilities. She deals with long-term planning and acquisition to supply ongoing manufacturing operations at multiple facilities. If her team fails to do their job, it can cause massive repercussions throughout the entire manufacturing supply chain.

When Bruce began working with Mary, half her team was new at their job and the pace of operations was so intense they simply didn't have the bandwidth to get their new people fully trained and up to speed. Experienced people were already showing signs of burnout due to shouldering the increased workload and, as they saw it, they simply didn't have time for training the new folks. Meanwhile, new people were growing more impatient and disengaged by the day. In fact, Mary had already spotted some looking for jobs online.

When Bruce asked her about her plan to get everyone on the team up to speed and productive, she said she was going to train all the new people herself. She simply didn't feel it was right to ask her experienced team members to conduct training on top of their already heavy workload. This makes perfect sense at one level, but this approach ran the risk of digging Mary further into the High Producer's Trap by taking her attention away from the more strategic needs of her operation.

Bruce instead persuaded Mary to take this challenge to the group as the focus of a Mini-Town Hall. Having run out of ideas of her own, she was willing to give it a try, and the more she talked through the process with Bruce, the more excited she became. She felt she was truly on the right path when she posed the idea to her team, and immediately had volunteers eager to help her plan and set up for the event.

Mary ran the idea by her boss, who knew full well that critical skill gaps like these were springing up across his directorate, as many of his most experienced people were part of the baby boom generation and were rapidly approaching retirement. He knew he had enormous skill gaps between his most and least experienced personnel, and traditional approaches to training did not entirely close these gaps. He was so intrigued by Mary's approach that he invited his own boss to her Mini-Town Hall and, while they initially planned to stay for only a short time, they both enjoyed the discussion so much they stayed through the entire meeting.

Over lunch and a brief icebreaker exercise, the working portion of the Mini-town Hall began with Mary's two bosses providing a view from the canopy. It is not often that employees are able to directly engage with the senior leaders of the organization. It is vital for people to see the operation from the canopy view, and conversely for leaders to understand life on the jungle floor. We therefore recommend senior leaders help launch these events while ensuring that they give employees appropriate space for open discussion and dialogue.

Her bosses explained how everyone was beginning to feel the early effects of a huge demographic shift as boomers were retiring in large numbers and taking their knowledge and experience with them. They emphasized how critical it was to the mission of the organization that they become highly adept at bringing new people on board and getting their skills rapidly up to speed. This also meant that everyone on her team, regardless of their experience level, kept their skills sharp and up-to-date. They emphasized that "A flexible employee is a valuable employee. If you master one skill, it is time to learn another," underscoring the need for cross-training and knowledge sharing.

With the team's attention now at its peak, Mary divided everyone into small groups and asked her team to discuss three basic questions:

- How can we keep our internal knowledge base current and improve how we share best practices within our team?

- How can we rapidly bring new people on board and help them become productive members of the team?

- How can we prepare all our team members for growth and advancement?

Mary and her bosses then stepped back, allowing the team to discuss these questions openly. Even those who were usually quiet in regular meetings were actively talking at their table. After a good deal of lively discussion and debate the team came together once again as a large group to discuss their ideas.

The team's plan was to do all the training themselves using subject matter experts (SME Trainers) derived largely from within their own organization. Each SME Trainer agreed to *own* a specific competency area. This included updating and maintaining all associated job aids, job breakdown sheets, and resources for each key competency area, bringing their institutional knowledge base up-to-date.

Each SME Trainer also agreed to train everyone on the team based on current best practices. SME Trainers could also choose to work as a team to develop the knowledge base for each competency area, promoting greater teamwork and knowledge sharing within the group.

Mary and her bosses began asking questions to draw out more details about the idea. Everyone in the room began contributing suggestions for what skills and competencies they all needed most. These were compiled into a set of user-friendly desktop guides for each competency area.

With their new guides in hand, the team agreed to meet every Thursday in a dedicated training room to receive hands-on, over-the-shoulder training from experienced team members who volunteered to become the first SME Trainers.

The SME Trainers recognized that there was something in it for them to fully embrace this process. They started by identifying specific lower-level tasks that were eating up their bandwidth. The sooner they could train the new team members on these tasks, the sooner they could get those tasks off their own plate. This allowed the most experienced team members to focus on more complicated aspects of the acquisition process, creating a win/win for everyone involved while making much better use of everyone's capabilities.

The team asked for more Mini-Town Halls, often inviting their colleagues from other parts of the organization to improve cross-functional coordination and integration of their processes. They solved many of their own cross-functional coordination issues this way and even had to request a bigger room for their training days because other groups wanted to participate!

Without Mary or her bosses telling them to do so, the team had created an Internal Development Path for themselves with specific steps toward their goals. Mary ensured that everyone who participated in the training received credit and that SME trainers received additional recognition for their important contributions. Newer people, eager to learn more, fully embraced this approach, and soon became productive members of the team.

Mary became reenergized, sharing with Bruce that her new goal was to work herself out of her job and position herself for the next level of management where she could mentor her staff—and teach them how to lead their own teams using this approach.

Closing the Knowledge Gap

We have found that the Internal Development Path closes a critical gap between explicit and tacit knowledge. While explicit knowledge can be codified in the form of manuals, databases, and training programs, tacit knowledge is a more refined form of know-how often concealed within the minds of individuals, teams, and communities of practice.

There is no one better to train others than the people who know the job best. While traditional forms of training remain important to the transfer of codified institutional knowledge, our experience has shown that these programs can be significantly augmented through the Internal Development Path as a means of cultivating tacit knowledge within organizations.

Lasting success can only be achieved when training, recognition, and rewards are aligned with the vision. Knowledge workers need to be involved in the changes that affect them. They want to learn, grow, and develop their skills. They want equal measures of autonomy and teamwork, and they want the ability to develop and share best practices. They also want recognition and rewards tied to their efforts—this is organizational currency for them.

The best people want to continually learn, develop their skills, and become more marketable. We, therefore, strongly suggest you tie rewards and recognition to the Internal Development Path, ensuring that employee goals remain aligned with those of the organization. This forges a connection between training and career advancement that can take on a life of its own, creating a wellspring of new ideas and innovative thinking throughout your organization. As we tell all our clients: it is like uncorking a genies bottle—just be careful where you point it!

Integrator Leader Reflections

- Are you creating the space for your team to self-organize behind the mission?

- Are you listening actively and building off their ideas?

- Are you thinking out loud with your team?

CHAPTER NINE

Where To Put Your Crowbar

"Give me a lever long enough and a fulcrum upon which to place it, and I will move the world."
Archimedes

We will now explore how to identify *where to put your crowbar* to gain maximum leverage for your change efforts. These are high-impact ideas, such as proposals for new products and services or process improvement initiatives, that require greater focused attention and effort. You will also learn what to do with a disillusioned team and get them rapidly back on track. These techniques will help you launch your change initiative with maximum impact and sustain it over time. You will see that the Mini-Town Hall is not intended to be a one-time event, but rather an approach to leading and engaging teams that you can use routinely throughout your organization.

Visible follow-up and follow-through are the keystones of any change process. These activities close the FEEDBACK LOOP that began when you first asked your team for their input. If you do not plan to follow through, it is better not to embark on this process in the first place, as you will breed cynicism in your team, diminishing the likelihood that they will take you seriously in the future. Conversely, when people see the impact of their ideas in motion, it builds trust and momentum in the team, encouraging them to engage more proactively in the change process.

Leading Change in a Multi-Billion Dollar Enterprise

Describing himself as "a simple farm kid from southern Michigan," Travis was now a senior leader who had risen through the ranks based on his reputation as a pragmatic, hands-on manager who was not afraid to jump in and get things done. He had a thorough and grounded knowledge of the operation where he and his team of two managers and 20 staff tracked billions of dollars in assets for their global organization.

Travis' team knew they could count on him for answers because he had vast knowledge of the enterprise and years of experience on the ground at the operational level. Yet Travis would frequently become frustrated with his team, and it showed. He confided in Bruce that he felt he had to shoulder too much of the day-to-day operational burden, and his staff simply wasn't always able to keep up. One of his managers was brand-new, and the other was not good at engaging with his own team, so Travis felt he had to step in to fill the gap himself. This left much of the organization feeling increasingly frustrated and disempowered.

To make matters worse, Travis had been tasked with a large project to bring all inventory up to a new set of operational and audit standards. He said his bandwidth was so consumed by the day-to-day operations that he didn't know how he and his team would manage this new and complex initiative on top of their regular work. He was feeling overwhelmed, and he knew his frustration was showing, which in turn affected the morale of his team. Travis was in a classic High Producer's Trap and needed a way out.

Travis's new initiative was a perfect opportunity to use the Mini-Town Hall. After a bit of coaching from Bruce, he initiated a series of these sessions focused on designing and deploying the new initiative. He used the Change Integrator model as a framework for the meeting, first outlining WHAT needed to be done and including key milestones and deadlines that they needed to meet. He then explained WHY the initiative was important to their customer, their operation, and to them personally. He then asked his team to figure out HOW best to accomplish the mission.

Travis said that the first meeting got off to a bit of an awkward start, and he later realized the team expected him to tell them HOW he wanted them to tackle the initiative. Instead, he was asking them HOW. Eventually one person spoke up, then another, and soon everyone was building off one another's ideas so much that it was hard for Travis to keep up. He filled several automated white boards with ideas from the team, which allowed him to quickly print out and post their reflections around the meeting room.

There were a few times he said the team "got a bit sidetracked chasing an idea down a rabbit hole." At these points, Travis would suggest that the idea be placed in *The Parking Lot* for discussion at another time. He then explored *where to put the crowbar* by prioritizing the input of his team into three basic categories: 1) Low-Hanging Fruit, 2) Parking Lot, and 3) High Priority. The team agreed to execute on all low-hanging fruit items as quickly as possible and assigned goal completion dates to each item. Then they agreed that items in *The Parking Lot* should be captured for later consideration. This left the team with the *High Priority* goals, which would become the primary focus of their time and effort moving forward.

The team began using the Mini-Town Hall as their default approach to their subsequent meetings about the audit initiative. To promote team autonomy and ownership of the project, Travis attended some of these meetings and chose not to attend others.

Of course, it wasn't always smooth sailing for Travis personally. He had to be careful not to fall back into the High Producer's Trap by solving problems that emerged along the way. Rather, he was determined that his team would be less dependent on him over time by learning to think strategically for themselves.

Travis kept a picture of the Change Integrator model on the wall behind his desk. It was an enduring reminder for everyone to work together to come up with alternatives rather than bringing problems to him. It reminded his team that they ultimately need to own the solutions.

Travis soon realized that the Mini-Town Hall was not merely a way of meeting, but rather it was a way of leading. He felt that, by sharing responsibility for driving change, an enormous weight had been taken off his shoulders. With his managers and their teams taking more ownership of the operational details, he now had bandwidth to think more strategically. His managers in turn learned how to use this process to lead their own teams. Many of the employees commented how much they appreciated this new collaborative approach and the opportunity to learn, share ideas, and be more involved in the decision-making process.

Defining Your Crowbar Goals

To determine *your own crowbar goals*, keep groups at their breakout tables in your Mini-Town Hall, facilitate discussions by going table-by-table to capture everyone's thoughts, and then categorize and prioritize outputs from the small group discussions with the help of the entire group.

First, eliminate any duplicate ideas, but make note of how often these ideas emerge because this indicates a pattern is emerging. Make three columns on the whiteboard with the following headings:

1. Low-Hanging Fruit

2. Parking Lot

3. High Priority

1. Low-hanging fruit — Quick to accomplish, visible and immediate impact

Ask the larger group to help you identify items on the whiteboard that could be implemented either immediately or within a week or so. Move all the items that fit these criteria in your list under this category. These are changes that can be put in place soon, and we highly encourage you to do just that.

The sooner you can demonstrate that you have listened to their ideas and put them in motion, the quicker you will build momentum. Many of us go our whole life never having a boss who truly listens to our ideas, let alone acts on them. Often these changes can have the most dramatic impact on morale. Once you've acted on these ideas and your team begins to see the impact on their daily activities, this will stimulate more ideas and more input.

2. Parking lot—Actions to be considered at a later date; have potential but outside current scope

This category is the opposite of low-hanging fruit. These are ideas that, while they may have merit, might be extremely costly or complex to implement. Nonetheless, ideas placed in this category may indicate a longer-term goal or trajectory for your organization. We certainly want to capture these ideas and hold them for a later time. If certain ideas in this category turn into long-term goals, then make sure to identify them as such and ensure that your short- and medium-term goals are in alignment with this longer-term trajectory.

3. High priority—Crowbar goals that need more focused effort

What is left in your list should now be high-priority ideas. This list will become the focus of the remainder of your group session. These are high-leverage, high-impact ideas that create what we call the *crowbar effect*. They normally take more focused effort and time but have the potential to yield significant results.

For example: Assume that you have 15 items remaining in your list that fall under the high-priority category. The problem is that 15 items do not constitute 15 priorities. You want to narrow this list generally to no more than three to five items. As the saying goes, if everything is a priority, then nothing is.

Prioritizing Through Multi-Voting

To engage the group in narrowing this list to a manageable size, give everyone three to five sticky notes and have them write their name on each one. Ask everyone to choose their top three to five priorities and allow them to discuss their choices amongst themselves. Once the discussions begin to die down, ask everyone to come up to the front of the room and place their votes on the high-priority items that had been written on the whiteboard. They can place all their sticky notes on one item if they so choose, or spread them out amongst their top three to five priorities. Now, step back and behold the pattern that emerges.

The beauty of this exercise, simple as it is, is that participants have taken part in the process of prioritizing the changes they feel will have the greatest impact on the efficiency and effectiveness of their operation. Once everyone votes, everyone can see the pattern that emerges as sticky notes cluster around certain ideas.

Remember, it is important to act as quickly as possible on all Low-Hanging Fruit items, ensuring that completion goal dates are assigned to each. Items in the Parking Lot, while perhaps having merit, may be too far outside the scope or current resources of the organization, and as such they need to be captured but moved aside for later discussion. This allows you and the team to focus on the high-priority crowbar goals in the list.

It is important that participants leave the meeting with a focused and clear path of action. There should be no doubt in their mind when they leave this meeting what they will begin working on. Before you conclude the session, conduct a short debriefing by asking everyone to discuss the following three questions:

- What worked well in this meeting?

- What worked least well in this meeting?

- What can we do differently in future meetings to make them more productive and engaging?

Capture all their ideas and consider incorporating their suggestions into future Mini-Town Hall meetings. Better yet, ask if anyone would like to volunteer to organize the next meeting. This will help to build a sense of initiative and ownership in the team, while encouraging them to use this process on their own.

Visible Follow-Up and Follow Through

After the Mini-Town Hall concludes, post the team's suggestions in your office (or in another highly visible area, internal blog, etc.) so that everyone can see that you are thinking about their comments and taking them seriously.

Do not delay taking immediate and visible action on all Low-Hanging Fruit items, as these help to create quick wins for the team. Next, focus on your High-Priority *crowbar goals* by allocating resources, defining outcome-based success criteria, key milestones, and completion dates. For your highest-priority initiatives, you may want to form Action Teams, a topic we will explore further in Chapter 11.

One client we worked with in an aerospace manufacturing facility chose, at the request of the team, to put a large bulletin board on a prominent wall at the intersection of several hallways where people walked by frequently. This soon became a place for people to stop, mingle, and discuss progress on their organizational goals. When an initiative was completed, the team heading the initiative would put a large red checkmark next to that item on the bulletin board. There were also areas for people to add additional ideas or to post comments. Many of our clients use an internal blog for this purpose, a powerful tool for communication with your team and a must if you have a distributed workforce.

Building Agility into Your Change Effort

Throughout all our research and experience, we have found that no matter how good the plans are that we create in advance, we are bound to encounter unforeseen obstacles and challenges, particularly in a VUCA world. Yet if we try to prepare for every potential scenario up front, we would be paralyzed and would never act. Instead, we must remain focused on our mission while remaining flexible in our tactics for achieving it.

While planning is important, we must not allow our plans to become a straitjacket that inhibits tactical flexibility in how we accomplish them. Referring to the Change Integrator, we must always distinguish WHAT we intend to accomplish from HOW we accomplish it.

When unforeseen events arise—which they invariably will—many teams may put blinders on, ignoring the facts on the ground, and charge ahead with the original plan. If we are not careful, deviation from the plan can be equated with failure. Yet true failure occurs when we don't appropriately sense and respond to shifting conditions on the ground, which can lead to the derailing of your initiative and the demoralizing of your team. This can initiate a vicious cycle where team members begin to point fingers at one another and attempt to assign blame for what went wrong, rather than focusing on finding a new path forward.

Therefore, it is critical that you begin the deployment of your initiative with these risks in mind up front. That way, when unforeseen challenges arise, your team will be prepared to take appropriate corrective action to get the initiative back on track.

Whenever an initiative begins to go sideways, your first step as an Integrator Leader should always be to look in the mirror at yourself—and ensure all the leaders in your operation do the same. Paraphrasing Mahatma Gandhi, *we need to become the change we seek in our organizations.* In other words, walk the talk, live by your values, and make sure all your team leaders are doing the same.

Leveraging Ambiguity to Drive Innovation

When things fail to go according to plan, the tendency is to make impulsive decisions that create the illusion of progress but may run counter to our long-term goals. It is important that you demonstrate agility from the top by pausing to listen to your people, make appropriate course corrections based on their input, and rally the troops to charge up the hill from another direction.

In times of uncertainty and ambiguity, do not make the mistake of confusing decisiveness with good decision-making. Rather than coming to premature closure on a path forward, the Integrator Leader must focus on creating a space within which team members can learn to *leverage ambiguity and uncertainty to drive innovation.* It is within the space of ambiguity and uncertainty that the field of possibility arises. The moment a decision is made, this field of possibility, innovation, and creativity collapses. [26]

If you are lost in the jungle, find the tallest tree and climb it. This view from the canopy will help your team regain their bearings, assess where they are in relation to their goal, and help them make the best decisions to move ahead.

In the industrial age, this canopy view of the operation was reserved for senior leaders. Yet, to be successful today, everyone must understand the mission, how their activities support it, and what they need from one another to succeed. Without the view from the canopy, the highly-specialized knowledge worker will invariably sub-optimize, making decisions that make sense at their level, but that may run counter to the organization's strategic direction.

A fundamental role of the Integrator Leader is to help the team overcome this internal fragmentation by routinely using Mini-Town Hall events to give them the view from the canopy and help them to self-organize behind the mission. Helping the team to maintain their bearings in this way may be all you need to do to keep your change initiative on track.

Just Enough, Just-in-Time Intervention

A word of caution here: *when missteps occur, don't take the problem back.* This will only demoralize your team, causing them to throw up their hands, give up, and be more dependent on you moving forward. This is like digging yourself further into the Founder or High Producer's Trap.

Instead, exercise what we call *just enough, just-in-time in-*

tervention. Use the techniques presented in this book to think aloud with your team about what happened: what worked, what didn't, what they need to do differently, and what they need from each other to overcome their challenges. Help them solve their own problems and, as much as possible, let it be their solution—not yours. As you help them break through these initial barriers, they will feel a renewed sense of vigor and optimism and will be less dependent upon you as a leader going forward.

Said another way, be careful not to jump in too quickly to rescue the group. This can easily be perceived as taking over the reins, implying that you do not have confidence in your team to resolve the more difficult challenges. If you do not show confidence in your people, future attempts to launch initiatives may fail to gain critical altitude. Your team will continue to rely on you for the answers, perpetuating an unhealthy culture of dependency.

At the same time, we don't want the initiative to languish too long and fall into a vicious cycle of blame, finger-pointing, and further disillusionment. The zone between disillusionment and breakthrough is a critical learning and developmental experience for the team. Be careful to balance the perceived need to intervene in the group with the need for the group to struggle a bit, to learn and grow through the experience of overcoming the obstacles they face on their own. The more the team feels they have succeeded on their own, the more confident they will become to take on even greater challenges in the future.

By doing this, your job as a leader will get easier, your team will become more competent and confident, your organization will become more efficient and resilient, and your customers will be more satisfied with the solutions you provide them.

Overcoming Resistance to Change

Maintaining change over time is not easy because resistance doesn't dissipate readily. You may experience success in the early stages of an initiative, but there may be cynical managers and employees that will look for opportunities to derail progress. Be aware that your team's early efforts will be fragile and can be undone with amazing speed.

Some recalcitrant leaders may need to be coached to improve their ability to communicate and reinforce the new strategic direction with their teams. If these leaders cannot change their own behavior, they may not be the right fit for the organization going forward. Because leaders set the example for their employees, they must be held to a high standard. You must identify problems early and provide them with appropriate feedback and coaching. When necessary, remove them before they have the chance to negatively impact the morale of the team and the success of the initiative.

To keep your finger on the pulse of the operation, continue to engage often with your teams using the Mini-Town Hall Scan process. This will help you and your team to rapidly identify and solve emerging problems and to take advantage of unforeseen opportunities along the way.

Lasting success cannot be achieved if human resource systems and programs are not aligned with the new direction. While you might achieve some results in the short term, if you fail to align incentives, recognition, and rewards with the new vision, the effort will eventually be undermined by the reward systems in place.

All hiring, compensation, and performance evaluation systems need to align with your efforts. Promotion decisions need to be made so that employees see that those who embrace the changes are rewarded with opportunities for advancement. Recruiting and hiring decisions must reflect the skills and characteristics that support your strategic priorities. Always provide people ample opportunity to develop their skills and potential to advance.[27]

Integrator Leader Reflections

- Are you following through on your crowbar initiatives using just enough, just-in-time leadership?

- Are you building agility into how you deploy change by listening to your team and helping them solve their own problems?

- Are you becoming the change you seek in your organization, while ensuring that all your team leaders are doing the same?

CHAPTER TEN

Leading Virtual Teams

"Trust. Clarity. Vision. Focus on these to make your virtual
team more effective."

George Bradt

Today's organizations are increasingly composed of individuals
and teams that are geographically dispersed. Whether you lead a
team of individuals who telecommute part of the week or an entirely distributed organization, Integrator Leaders need to adapt
their leadership approach to ensure their distributed workforce
can achieve superior results.

This chapter will explore how distributed teams can learn to
self-organize behind mission priorities, resulting in greater customer satisfaction, organization effectiveness, and employee engagement. You will learn how to treat your distributed workers
just as if they were sitting in the office with you, making them an
integral part of the team. Our goal is to create a more cohesive
team that can collaborate across space, time, and organization
boundaries to align behind mission priorities while requiring
less direct supervision.

Principles of Virtual Leadership

Based on our decades of research and experience with virtual teams,[28] we have found the same principles that are important for leading an on-site team are even more critical for leading a virtual team. These include the following:

- **Trust**: Leaders must create a climate of mutual trust between themselves and those they lead virtually, including a climate of trust between team members. Trust becomes firmly grounded within a team that upholds strong values.

- **Vision**: The leader must create a clear and compelling vision for their organization. It is this compass heading that helps the team members prioritize and align their efforts in support of the mission.

- **Communication**: Regular communication between the leader and all virtual-team members is essential. It is equally important for team members to communicate between themselves without the leader's involvement. This ensures that the team is learning to self-organize and self-correct behind mission priorities.

- **Accountability**: All members of the team must be held accountable for outcomes, not merely their inputs. That is, while everyone must be held to the same high standard of individual performance, they must also be held accountable for the outcome they achieve.

- **Feedback**: Timely, actionable feedback is critical when managing a team in the virtual world. This allows immediate course correction if a team member is underperforming, helping them to make necessary changes to improve their performance.

- **Recognition**: As meaningful as it is to recognize performance face-to-face, with virtual teams this is often impossible. The key is to provide timely recognition for individual and team performance. This is even more important when your team is distributed. Consider a posting on an internal blog or team email. Everyone then has a permanent record of an accomplishment they can refer to at any time. A follow-up with a formal award is also important, but this digital method of rapidly showing recognition is well-received today.

The Virtual Stand-Up Meeting

The Virtual Standup Meeting is a process for promoting self-organization, dialogue, and alignment in your team. Our goal here is to get your geographically dispersed team to engage with each other regularly, as though they worked in the same office. To get them to do so, we suggest that you intentionally place time constraints that inhibit dialogue *on the call*, while promoting more team engagement *prior to the call*. This also helps to develop team discipline by having everyone summarize key points ahead of time in concise headline form.

Schedule a call for *all* team members, those on-site and geographically dispersed. Ask that on-site participants dial in for this call from their desk to even the playing field for all team members. Ensure that everyone participates—make it mandatory.

Prepare a meeting agenda and ask that each team member provide their concise input to a specific topic, task, or project. Send this agenda with your proposed discussion topics out a day or more in advance to give everyone a chance to prepare for the meeting. Tell the team that you only have ten minutes for the call; therefore, it is critical to begin and finish up exactly on time, whether or not everyone has completed their remarks. If you have a very large group, you may require more than ten minutes, but if you keep these principles in mind, you will still achieve the desired outcome—a more engaged team that becomes less dependent on you over time.

Begin the meeting by briefly reviewing the purpose and ground rules for the meeting. Ask each person to provide their input concisely. No one is permitted to say that they merely agree with the person before them.

After each person provides their input, simply say "thank you" and call on the next person. Don't permit discussion. Schedule another time for more dialogue on a specific topic or make it a point to follow up later with a call to specific individuals.

Exactly at the ten-minute mark, politely thank the team and end the call. If necessary, repeat this exercise two or three times in the same manner, always with a new topic.

Ideally, after the first or second call the team will realize that time is short, and they could benefit by discussing these topics between themselves in advance. If this occurs, congratulations! If it does not, prior to the third call, explain to the team that you want them to discuss the topic between themselves prior to the call so that they can build off each other's ideas and their collective input can be more aligned and focused. By continuing this practice, the result will be a more cross-functionally aligned and cohesive team.

Leaving the Virtual Room

On the next call, the Integrator Leader needs to leave the room. That is, rather than ending the call, the leader should exit the call after initiating the meeting. Gather your team on the call and prepare them to discuss current priority initiatives, best practices, or share problem areas with their peers. Set the tone and expectations and provide the space (virtual call), and have the team engage in HOW to solve problems. Once the discussion is underway, let the team know that you will be signing off the call temporarily, and give them a designated time you will reengage with them.

Remind your team that we are each good at something, but no one is good at everything. Therefore, just like you are seeking their input, they must share between themselves to develop effective solutions. Let them know you expect each member of the team to communicate with one another regularly. Ask them to go to each other when they come across a problem, and if they encounter a challenge they are unable to solve or that requires additional resources, come to you collectively—bringing potential alternatives and solutions.

While you are out of the virtual room, your team should share challenges, best practices, and observations. Keeping within the vision and the boundaries provided, they should discuss what they need from each other to accomplish the mission. They should learn from each other, building trust and confidence while growing less dependent on you.

When you return to the call, ask for their input on the topic at hand, using the principles and techniques we provided for you earlier in this book to engage with your team. The ideal we are constantly working toward is to engage virtually with your team just as if you were in the same room with them. Remember that regardless of how sophisticated the technology you use, in the end this is only a medium for what otherwise remains a process of human social engagement.

Building Trust and Engagement in a Virtual Team

Jackie was a highly successful human resources leader with 18 years in the business. She had just been selected by the CEO from a pool of candidates to run her company's demanding western regional health services recruiting team.

Her region covered 11 western states and her office was co-located with one of her four subordinate satellite offices in Denver. While each of her managers were highly motivated, most of them lacked experience in the health services recruiting field. Three of the managers had been in place for about 12-18 months, while one was entirely new to the job.

While coaching Jackie, Jim suggested that she travel to meet with each of her satellite office managers right away to get to know each of them individually. They both agreed this was essential for her to build a foundation of trust between herself and her team.

Jackie was convinced that the same values that earned her a sterling reputation in her previous position, like mutual trust and respect, open communication, holding people accountable, giving praise and recognizing a job well done, would continue to guide her forward. She simply needed new ways to engage with her team—and get them to engage with one another—in a virtual environment.

She learned that her predecessor had been only partially successful in meeting her personnel recruitment targets. The performance of each office varied widely, indicating that they were not sharing best practices amongst themselves. Each manager was so focused on meeting their individual goals that they rarely took the time to reach out to engage with one another. Although the regional headquarters had staff and resources available to support them, the satellite offices rarely sought their assistance because they felt that it was more trouble than it was worth—a bureaucratic paper drill that just wasted their time.

Through her work with Jim, Jackie realized that she had to first help her team learn to see her region more as an integrated whole rather than a collection of regional offices. As she put it, "We have to get them to see themselves as one team paddling in the same direction." This became Jackie's primary goal as leader of the organization. Jackie asked Jim to assist her to develop a modified Mini-Town Hall to help her to get her team to self-organize behind her intent to accomplish their mission, ultimately achieving her goal.

Jackie's solution to promote more cross-functional dialogue was to implement what Jim described as the *10-minute virtual stand-up call*. She told her managers that she would conduct these meetings twice monthly by phone to gain input on specific issues from them. The focus of the first call was to identify the region's top strengths and challenges.

Although one of her managers (co-located with her at the regional office) offered to conduct the call from his office, she politely declined. Though it would have been more convenient, she did not want to appear to be giving him preferential treatment. Several team members told her later that they appreciated this gesture as a means of keeping everyone on a level playing field during the meetings.

When it was time for the first call, exactly on schedule, Jackie dialed in. She quickly reinforced the meeting rules: calls begin and end on schedule; one speaker at a time; be prepared and concise since time is limited; and no one is permitted to say that they merely agree with the person before them. After each manager stated their perception of the strengths and challenges facing the region, Jackie simply said thank you, intentionally avoiding a lengthy discussion on the topic. Because their perceptions of their strengths and challenges as a region varied dramatically, it confirmed her initial suspicion that they were not engaging with one another as a team.

At the end of the ten minutes, she thanked everyone for their input and told them that the topic for the next call was to provide the names of the three most important stakeholders for the region and why. They typically focused their recruiting efforts on universities, hospitals, and clinics, and she was curious if her managers had identified any unique resources in their respective area of operation.

The second session went much like the first. Once again, she could tell that the managers were simply reacting to her request and providing their personal thoughts without engaging with one another first.

During a meeting with her San Diego manager, Jackie asked

her how often she spoke with the other three managers. "Almost never, we are too busy for that," she said. Then Jackie asked if she sought help from anyone on her own team in providing responses to the 10-minute stand-up meetings. Seeming a bit surprised and almost a bit offended at the question, her manager responded, "No one gave me input, those are my ideas. I know what's going on in my office."

This provided the perfect coaching opportunity. Jackie knew that one of her other managers had already solved a problem that the San Diego branch was now experiencing. She suggested that the two managers meet and then share what they learn with the other managers.

Jackie also encouraged the manager to engage with her own team prior to each stand-up call. Not only would the manager obtain valuable input, but it would help her team feel valued, strengthen the organization, and make her job as a manager easier. As she frequently felt overwhelmed, this last point really got her attention. This small amount of just enough, just-in-time coaching helped the manager to see her own role as a leader differently. She realized that she did not have to have all the answers and that involving her team would be better for everyone.

At the next 10-minute stand-up call, one manager told Jackie that they might not need ten minutes that day because he was able to provide a collective response. All the managers had worked together prior to the call.

This is exactly what Jackie was looking for. The San Diego manager had reached out to the others, and each had discussed the stand-up meeting with their own internal team. The managers then participated in a series of teleconferences to discuss what they had each learned from their teams. Together they came up with a plan for Jackie that was comprehensive and aligned directly with the specific goals that she had laid out for her region.

At that point, Jackie knew her team was finally beginning to paddle in the same direction. They even asked if they could meet quarterly at a different satellite office location to learn from one another and to see their region through the perspectives of their peers.

Over the coming months, the morale and performance of Jackie's team improved. New ideas and best practices began to emerge from the team's virtual interactions that strengthened the entire region. Jackie told Jim that learning to lead virtual teams this way had not only made her team more effective, but her own job was becoming easier and more enjoyable.

Guiding the Ship from the Virtual Helm

Techniques like the 10-Minute Standup Meeting allow you as an Integrator Leader to guide the ship from the virtual helm while keeping your finger on the pulse of your organization. As we see from the story of Jackie and her team above, you should expect and encourage your team to go to each other first for answers before coming to you. Recognize team members for their individual contributions while helping them to see how their ideas fit into the view from the canopy proactively identifying what they need from one another to fulfill their mission.

Remember, knowledge workers are specialists who know more and more about less and less. Therefore, their individual ideas, while likely to have merit, must be integrated into a cohesive approach in support of the mission. Rather than attempting to "manage" the organization, the Integrator Leader focuses on creating the conditions for people to self-organize behind the mission within the boundaries of their intent.

Asynchronous Digital Collaboration

Asynchronous collaboration tools known as *groupware* work well for teams that must collaborate over space and time for an extended period. If your organization is creating a new product or service, deploying a new initiative, or simply needs to collaborate more effectively over space and time, these tools can be invaluable.

These tools can be as simple as a threaded discussion list or an internal blog, and as advanced as online communities of practice or Action Teams (see chapter 11) that engage together over extended periods of time. Bruce taught graduate school for nearly two decades using collaborative web-based tools, allowing him to teach students all over the world regardless of their time zone or physical restrictions.[29]

A key benefit of groupware is that all online conversations are captured and can be arranged in ways that allow for more in-depth reflection, discussion, and dialogue among leader and team members, and between team members themselves. An enduring record is generated, including all shared discussion threads, documents, and resources. In addition, people can think through their contribution before posting, and even less assertive individuals can step up and be heard and engaged.

While there are scores of digital video and web-based collaboration platforms to choose from, many of our clients around the world operate where high-speed connectivity is not always available. Cyber security concerns may also preclude the use of some popular collaboration platforms. We encourage you to do your research and use the appropriate collaboration platform for your purposes.

Virtual Feedback and Leader Development

When leading in a virtual environment we must create ways to make up for the lack of routine face-to-face interaction. As an Integrator Leader, and especially as a leader of a virtual team, you can't over-communicate. Keep in mind that a key part of communicating is listening. We, therefore, recommend that you regularly solicit your team for input on your performance and ideas. One way of doing this is to use 360 multi-source feedback surveys where the leader receives input from peers, direct reports, superiors, and other stakeholders. Organizational culture surveys can also be useful tools to obtain an overall barometer on the organization from the perspective of employees and external stakeholders.

Leading and working virtually has its benefits in the freedom and flexibility it affords both the employee and the employer. We believe it is also a good part of any sensible resiliency plan, ensuring that all essential functions of your company can continue in the face of natural or man-made disaster, or even severe weather where people cannot or should not commute to work. However, a downside is that the lack of face-time with colleagues and leaders in the organization can lead to a sense of invisibility, where employees working virtually could be left out of decision-making or passed over for promotion.

Don't hesitate to bring your own boss to selected virtual meetings to showcase your team members by letting them present, discuss, and engage with the senior leaders of the organization. Use this as a way to highlight the talents of your team and to provide avenues for their development and advancement. These steps will help deepen trust and move your team from compliance to commitment.

Integrator Leader Reflections

- What are you doing to build a sense of trust and community in your virtual team?

- What are you doing to promote cross-functional communication, coordination, and integration in your virtual organization?

- How are you ensuring that each member of your virtual team feels included and engaged as a full member of the team?

CHAPTER ELEVEN

Leading Change with Action Teams

"Vision without action is merely a dream. Action without vision just passes the time. Vision with action can change the world."
Joel A. Barker

Action Teams are ideal for focusing on high-priority initiatives such as designing new products, launching new initiatives, and integrating critical cross-functional process gaps. By nature, Action Teams tend to be cross-functional and cross-organizational, drawing together individuals with specialized skills to collaborate on developing and applying new forms of knowledge to accomplish strategic goals.

The concept of Action Teams emerged from our extensive research and experience [30] about how the best teams perform under pressure to achieve extraordinary results. From these examples, we can learn lessons and distill basic principles for creating a culture that fosters innovation and a proactive approach to change.

Action Teams and the Informal Organization

If you *look the right way*, you may see that something akin to Action Teams already operates within your organization. Resembling communities of practice,[31] these groups comprise an informal organization that has learned how to overcome barriers imposed by formal structure, hierarchy, and procedures. Their guiding ethos appears to be the notion that organization charts are there to figure out who you have to work around to get the job done.

Because these groups are informal and tend to work under the radar, they may pose a threat to those who derive their legitimacy through formal rank and hierarchy. Hence, communities of practice are rarely formally sanctioned. As such, they tend to be ad hoc, under-resourced, and underutilized.

Action Teams tap into the latent operational intelligence within the informal organization and channel it into mission priorities. Action Teams do not behave like automatons. They are not there simply to obey orders or follow a process, but to apply their skills, talents, and intelligence to meet a goal. Rather than providing the Action Teams detailed battle plans, provide your strategic intent (WHAT) and your rationale (WHY) and charge them with developing the roadmap for HOW to get there. Move from over-defining objectives and the means of achieving them toward providing clear vision and parameters for the discretionary use of resources to achieve objectives.[32]

We suggest that you use the Focus version of the Mini-Town Hall to provide space for reflection on how to achieve intended outcomes. Clarify your vision, the boundaries within which they must act, and how their actions fit within your strategic intent. Ask the team to develop an action plan that outlines how they will move forward, always seeking to provide integrated solutions for your customer.

Action Teams and Cyber Defense

Randy was a highly accomplished IT security specialist. He had made a name for himself as someone who was skilled, knowledgeable, and knew how to get the job done. This caught the eye of upper management, and Randy was promoted into one of the most sensitive and critical jobs in a global organization, head of the Cyber Defense Team. The job was to protect some of the most highly sensitive and sought-after information in the world, and they were under constant threat of attack. A successful intrusion into the system would put at risk billions of dollars in intellectual property, physical assets, and human lives.

In the world of cyber warfare, your enemy may be wandering around stealthily in your midst—and you don't know it until the damage is done. Highly trained hackers, some state-sponsored and others rogue individuals, were constantly looking for vulnerabilities in the network. Randy and his team had to be right 100% of the time in order to stop these attacks, while their adversaries only had to get it right once to wreak havoc.

By all objective measures, Randy's team was doing very well. In fact, they had just won a major award for their superb response to a recent cyber intrusion and for saving several million dollars by developing sophisticated intrusion detection systems in-house.

As his leadership coaching sessions with Bruce progressed, Randy admitted that something still was not clicking with his team. Technically speaking, most of his people were among the very best, but meetings felt like going to the dentist. No one freely offered input; instead Randy felt like he had to extract insights from them. It was painful for everyone involved. Because

BRUCE LARUE & JIM SOLOMON

Randy struggled to get his team to engage, he found himself making up for the silence by doing most of the talking in meetings. He knew they could do much better, but he simply didn't know how to get them to the next level.

As part of his coaching with Bruce, Randy participated in a 360 multi-source feedback survey. The results indicated that everyone appreciated Randy as a personable and technically competent boss who didn't micromanage. However, he scored low on adaptability, change, and innovation. Further, the team didn't see a compelling vision for the future, leaving many people questioning whether they should invest themselves long-term in the organization.

The 360 survey indicated that Randy's team felt left out of improvement processes. They said that Randy spent too much time in his office and during meetings he often talked too much and did not give them enough time to develop their own solutions to problems. Some people even wondered whether he really wanted to lead the organization.

Clearly, there was a major disconnect between how the team saw Randy and how he perceived himself as their leader. Through his discussions with Bruce, Randy began to see his organization through new eyes and realized that part of the problem was his own leadership approach. Rather than seeing his team as disengaged or recalcitrant, he realized that they had a lot of pent-up energy and ideas but lacked a clear vision for the future and constructive ways to channel their frustration and creativity.

As we caution all our clients, Bruce warned Randy that—while an organization may attract the best and brightest people, they are also the first to leave if they do not feel that they are learning and developing their portfolio of skills. The people who remain stay for various reasons, but often may be less talented and have fewer career options. This is a growing *continuity of operations challenge* for many organizations today. If situations like this remain unchecked, you can rapidly lose your very best talent—and seed your competitive advantage to your rivals.

In fact, this was already beginning to happen, and Randy was very concerned about a further talent drain due to the relatively low morale of his team. In addition, he was concerned about the lure of outside opportunities drawing away his best people. Many members of his team seemed disengaged, especially on second and third shifts. Absenteeism had begun to creep up, another early indicator of low morale.

Randy further acknowledged to Bruce that there were critical skill gaps and inconsistencies in performance between shifts in their 24/7 operation. Yes, they were all current on their mandatory training and certifications. But we all know there are differences between those highly seasoned and experienced people and those who possess the technical knowledge but lack the refinement that comes from the crucible of time and experience. The question is, how do we get people to willingly share their knowledge and mentor others? A true transfer of highly specialized knowledge, insight, and wisdom only occurs voluntarily. We, as Integrator Leaders, can only create the conditions for it to occur.

Randy also admitted that he and his team existed in something of a bubble. Their network operations control center was a fortified bunker, protected by multiple layers of the most sophisticated biometric devices available. His team was technically among the best of the best, but Randy said, "We go from long stretches of mind-numbing boredom staring at screens, to moments of sheer terror that resemble a cyber rugby scrum. Everyone simultaneously attacks the ball, eliminates the threat, takes countermeasures, and after filing the after-action report, we all relapse back into long stretches of boredom."

Bruce challenged Randy to view the challenges he and his team were facing as symptoms of the lack of a clear and compelling vision for the future. He asked him to think about not just where he saw the organization today, but more importantly, where was it going from here? What was the compass heading for the future? What should the operation look like to be fit for purpose in a VUCA world? How could Randy help the team stay one step ahead of the next cyber intrusion? How could Randy keep the team sharp, vigilant, and at the cutting edge without boring them or burning them out? Finally, how could he attract, develop, and retain his top talent?

After exploring these questions with Bruce, Randy decided his goal was nothing less than to build a world-class Cyber Defense Team. Bruce and Randy then began exploring the key gaps between where the team was currently, and the direction he wanted to take them.

This led to a series of Mini-Town Hall meetings where Randy challenged the team with the question of HOW to become a world-class cyber defense team. Using the processes outlined earlier in this book, the team came up with a plan to create a virtual machine using an identical image of their system, isolated it from the network, and then formed competing Cyber Action Teams to try to break it.

Each team took turns competing against one another to come up with ways to attack the virtual machine, while the other teams tried to detect and eliminate the threat. They then pulled all the relevant log files, analyzed the results, and wrote an after-action report on their findings. They then used this information to improve their cyber defense strategy.

All participants received official credit for engaging in the cyber warfare exercises. Cyber Action Teams that developed a process improvement received a reward and had their names attached to the new process, which was then placed on an internal shared drive for everyone to use going forward. This recognition benefited their career and built a sense of stature amongst their peers that proved to be a tremendous morale boost. The win for their customer was also tremendous as they now had a far more engaged and innovative team constantly seeking vulnerabilities in their system and building robust defensive measures against potential cyber-attack.

Although some team members sat on the sidelines during the first cyber warfare exercises, they soon found themselves on the *outside looking in* as they watched their teammates thoroughly enjoying themselves, sharpening and honing each other's skills, and receiving recognition for their efforts. Because no one was compelled to participate, the cyber Action Teams developed a sense of pride in ownership of the initiative, and it is growing to become a recognized best practice in the industry.

How to Build Action Teams

When creating your Action Teams, first identify participants whose talent, skills, and input would be necessary to succeed in your initiative. Also consider all those who would be significantly affected by any proposed changes. Engage all relevant stakeholders early in the process to gain their input, build their trust, and seek their buy-in.

Typically, the Action Team will be comprised of key members of this stakeholder group. Others will only engage the process at critical touchpoints. Including all relevant stakeholders at the appropriate times will ensure that you receive valuable input while addressing the concerns of those who could otherwise resist the change.

Tie Rewards to Outcomes

Let participants know up front that their work as a member of the Action Team is important and compensate them accordingly. If they think they are just checking a box, they will trivialize the process. Use performance reviews and bonuses to reinforce appropriate behaviors and successful implementation of initiatives. Tie rewards to the successful outcome of the initiative, and not for just doing one's job![33]

Integrate Lessons Learned

Too often, what is learned from these initiatives is not disseminated. This leaves future Action Teams vulnerable to reinventing the wheel. Honestly evaluate what went well and what could be improved, using the questions that we explored previously in the Mini-Town Hall process.

Leaders who are overcommitted to well-worn scripts and "fighting according to plan" instead of allowing people to self-organize in support of the mission risk suffering embarrassing defeats. Action Teams can become the catalyst for transformational change in your organization.

Integrator Leader Reflections

- Have you provided clear intent and appropriate boundaries for your Action Team to determine HOW to achieve their mission?

- Does your Action Team include participants whose input would be necessary to succeed in your initiative?

- Have you tied appropriate recognition and rewards to the outcomes you want your Action Team to achieve?

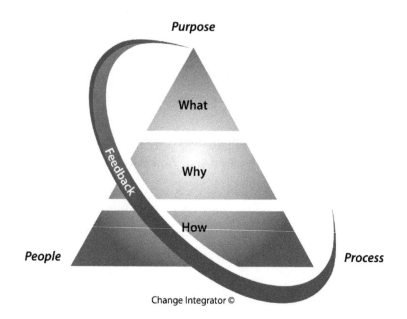

Change Integrator ©

The Future for Integrator Leaders

We hope this book has helped you to see your world in new ways and that you are inspired to help others do the same. The more you remain consistent with the Integrator Leader principles, techniques, and strategies we have explored in this book, the greater the results you will achieve.

Like everyone, you will face challenges, but you are now better equipped with principles and techniques to transform these challenges into opportunities for growth and development.

Now that you have learned to see possibilities where others see obstacles, you can inspire others with fresh visions of the future, while helping them align their efforts to make their shared vision a reality. Wherever you find yourself today, we encourage you to use this book as a field guide to create positive change in the world around you.

We hope the stories and examples we have shared have inspired you in your own learning process. Now we encourage you to share your own story of how you have applied what you have learned in this book with us at **www.chambersbayinstitute.com**.

Acknowledgements

We are grateful to all who have been an influence in our lives, have assisted in our own development, and who have helped us to learn to see in new ways.

We especially appreciate those whose stories we have shared in this book, as well as, the thousands of others who we have coached over the years. Our work with these leaders has helped immensely to refine our methodology through the crucible of real-world practice.

We tip our hat to our expert team at Chambers Bay Institute as they continually help us refine and validate our methodology through their work with thousands of leaders around the globe, inspiring them to see their world in new ways.

We give a special thank you to Brenda LaRue and Stephanie Galindo who had the patience, and discipline to edit our manuscript and provide needed constructive criticism along the way.

We also appreciate our team at Deed's Publishing for their instrumental advice and guidance to carry the ball across the finish line, making this book reality.

We are especially grateful to our spouses and families who have encouraged us to persevere to fulfill our vision for this book.

Finally, we are grateful to each other, for our walk together on this unfolding journey of learning to *see what isn't there...*

ABOUT THE AUTHORS

Bruce LaRue, PhD
President & Cofounder, Chambers Bay Institute

Bruce has focused much of his career on the emergence of the knowledge economy and its implications for the development of leadership competencies in distributed, technologically complex organizations. He has inspired thousands of leaders around the world *to see in new ways* while developing self-organizing Action Teams capable of transforming their vision into reality.

As a consultant, graduate professor, and coach, Bruce has worked with leaders in aerospace, the Department of Defense, wireless telecommunications, cyber security, global logistics, financial services, municipal and national government, and the nonprofit sector.

Jim Solomon

CEO & Cofounder, Chambers Bay Institute

Following his leader development studies at the University of North Georgia, Jim was commissioned and advanced in his Army career to the rank of Colonel with global responsibilities. He then went on to hold numerous leadership positions within Fortune 500 corporations, privately owned companies, and entrepreneurial startups. His spirit of service attracted him to volunteer on various non-profit boards where he has served as committee chairs and Chairman of one of the largest senior living communities in the state of Texas.

As a leadership coach, consultant, and author, Jim continues to demonstrate his commitment to developing capable leaders for future generations. Jim's leadership philosophy is simple - it's all about WE, not ME.

Bruce and Jim have collaborated on global projects, leadership coaching, and writings since 2004. Together they founded Chambers Bay Institute, where their mission is to develop leaders capable of leading *change in a complex world*.

To learn more about Chambers Bay Institute, visit **www.chambersbayinstitute.com**.

NOTES

1. For more on neural plasticity, see informative videos and publications at the University of Oregon Brain Development Lab. Helen J. Neville, Director, and her colleagues have developed a series of informative publications and videos about neural plasticity aimed at the lay audience. This emerging science has overturned the notion that the brain is somehow hardwired, and at some point becomes unchangeable. Instead, the brain develops much of its capacity based on experience, with a special emphasis placed on what are referred to as "sensitive periods" where the brain is especially susceptible to outside influence. For more information, see their videos and research at: http://changingbrains.org/.

   For a fascinating integration of Western neural science and the Buddhist tradition, see the work of Sharon Begley, *Train Your Mind, Change Your Brain: How a New Science Reveals Our Extraordinary Potential to Transform Ourselves* (New York: Ballantine Books, 2007). The book approaches the emerging science of neural plasticity through dialogues and research conducted by Western brain scientists in conjunction with the Dalai Lama and a group of Buddhist monks.

2. The University of North Georgia, one of the six United States senior military colleges (SMC) directed under 10 USC 2111a(f), is the state's Leadership Institution, and its Corps of Cadets has been recognized as having one of the country's best leader development programs. Jim is a graduate and was a four-year member of the Corps of Cadets. www.ung.edu

3. This example was first published in *Leading Organizations from the Inside Out: Unleashing the Collaborative Genius of Action-*

Learning Teams by Bruce LaRue, Paul Childs, and Kerry Larson. New York: John Wiley & Sons, 2006.

4. Consulting work performed on this initiative while Bruce was partner at Leadership Strategies International, Inc.

5. LaRue, Bruce. (2014). "Creating Broad Engagement in Change: Integrating Strategy & Action in Knowledge-Based Organizations." Chambers Bay Institute.

    Mini-Town Hall© is a process that was designed and developed by Chambers Bay Institute. Additional information regarding this innovative process may be found at www. chambersbayinstitute.com.

6. The concept of the integrator as a work style originated with Ichak Adizes, *Managing Corporate Lifecycles*, rev. and enl. ed. (Paramus, N.J.: Prentice Hall Press, 1999). More information can also be found on Dr. Adizes' website at www.adizes.com.

    The term *Integrator Leader* as we use it here focuses more on characteristics of a leadership style rather than a work style.

7. Bruce LaRue and Robert Ivany, "Transform Your Culture through Action-Learning Teams," *Executive Excellence Magazine*, December 2004, 14-15.

8. Ibid.

9. Bjarni Jonsson, "Public Communicative Engagement and Conscious Evolution of Human Social Systems," Third Generation Gravesians, 2013, accessed 2.21.18, http://www. graves3g.com/bjarni-1

    Bruce LaRue, "What Matters to Us in Life". YouTube video, 02:17. Posted November 1, 2009. https://www.youtube.com/ watch?v=5bSua_VD3Ms

10. For more on this concept, see: J. Krishnamurti, *Freedom from the Known*, 1st US ed. (New York: Harper & Row, 1969).

    J. Krishnamurti and David Bohm, *The Limits of Thought* (London, New York: Routledge, 1998).

    David Bohm, *Thought as a System* (London, New York: Routledge, 1994).

11. Bruce LaRue and Linda Shaffer-Vanaria, "Soft Focus: The New Edge of Mastery," *Leadership Excellence Magazine*, April 2005, 7. www.leaderexcel.com

12. See for example: Daniel Kahneman, *Thinking, Fast and Slow*, 1st pbk. ed. (New York: Farrar, Straus and Giroux, 2013). Kahneman, a Nobel laureate, outlines in vivid detail how humans systematically deceived themselves, creating false narratives and rationales for their actions. This is often due to what he calls the "What You See Is All There Is" bias, where humans systematically filter and narrow their field of vision, then take actions on the basis of this incomplete picture.

    See also: Jamie Holmes, *Nonsense: The Power of Not Knowing* (New York: Crown Publishers, 2015). Holmes outlines the dangers of leaders being unable to tolerate uncertainty, causing them to narrow their field of vision and shut out further information in favor of coming to premature closure on decisions, leading to suboptimal, if not disastrous, outcomes

    See also: Kevin McSpadden, "You Now Have a Shorter Attention Span Than a Goldfish," Time, May 14, 2015, http://time.com/3858309/attention-spans-goldfish/. The average attention span for "the notoriously ill-focused goldfish is nine seconds, but according to a new study from Microsoft Corp., people now generally lose concentration after eight seconds, highlighting the effects of an increasingly digitalized lifestyle on the brain."

13. Bruce LaRue, Dan Burden, Morel Fourman, Sarah Bowman, "Creating Sustainable, Resilient, and Livable Cities: A Call for Transformational Change" (presentation, 52nd International Making Cities Livable Conference on Achieving Green, Healthy Cities & Design Awards Competition on Designing for Green, Healthy Cities, Bristol, UK, June 29 - July 3, 2015). http://www.livablecities.org/conferences/52nd-conference-bristol

14. See for example: Walter Isaacson's *Steve Jobs* (New York: Simon & Schuster, 2011). Isaacson used the term reality distortion field to describe the late Steve Jobs' uncanny ability to consciously see the world in new and novel ways, and in so doing, create conditions for the development of innovative products and services. As it refers to the prison of the known, it describes an unconscious distortion of reality caused by the influence of culture on the human mind.

15. Ichak Adizes, *Managing Corporate Lifecycles*, rev. and enl. ed. (Paramus, N.J.: Prentice Hall Press, 1999).

16. Bruce LaRue, Kerry Larson, and Mark Sobol were partners in Leadership Strategies International Inc. which consulted on this initiative.

17. See for example: D. Michael Abrashoff, *It's Your Ship: Management Techniques from the Best Damn Ship in the Navy*, 2nd ed. (New York: Business Plus, 2012). Captain Abrashoff led the crew of an Aegis Class destroyer from one of the worst performing to highest performing ships in the Navy's Fifth Fleet, in large part by instilling an ownership mentality in the crew.

18. LaRue, Childs, and Larson, *Leading Organizations from the Inside Out*, 2nd ed. Portions of the current volume were excerpted and modified from chapter 7, pp. 110-120.

19. Bruce LaRue, Kerry Larson, and Mark Sobol were partners in Leadership Strategies International, Inc. which consulted on this initiative.

20. Laurie Kulikowski, "The 10 Largest IPOs of U.S. Companies on Record," The Street, July 23, 2016, https://www.thestreet.com/slideshow/13649641/1/the-10-largest-ipos-of-u-s-companies-on-record.html

21. All further details withheld for confidentiality purposes.

22. Laura Woods, "Elon Musk's Best Tips for Aspiring Entrepreneurs," GOBankingRates, May 25, 2017, https://www.gobankingrates.com/making-money/money-moves-elon-musks-business-playbook/

23. James C. Collins, *Good to Great: Why Some Companies Make the Leap and Others Don't*, Audiobook, performed by James Collins (2001; New York: Harper Audio), 2005.

24. Kim Malone Scott, *Radical Candor: Be a Kick-Ass Boss Without Losing Your Humanity*, Audiobook, performed by Kim Scott (2017; New York: Macmillan Audio), 2017.

25. P.F. Drucker, *Management Challenges for the 21st Century* (New York: Harper Business, 1999).

26. See for example: Jamie Holmes, *Nonsense: The Power of Not Knowing*, 1st ed. (New York: Crown Publishers, 2015). An excellent book for a window into the psyche of how effective leaders make decisions by tolerating ambiguity and remaining open to relevant input until the decision must be made, while others tend to come to premature closure on decisions due to their inability to tolerate ambiguity and uncertainty.

27. LaRue, Childs and Larson, *Leading Organizations from the Inside Out*, chapter 4.
   LaRue, Bruce. (2014). "Creating Broad Engagement in Change: Integrating Strategy & Action in Knowledge-Based Organizations." Chambers Bay Institute.

28. Bruce LaRue and Jim Solomon, "Leading Virtual Teams," *Creating High Performing Teams in Distributed Organizations* (University Place, WA: Chambers Bay Institute, 2017).

29. LaRue, Bruce, and Stephanie Galindo. "Synthesizing Corporate and Higher Education Learning Strategies." Handbook of Online Learning : Innovations in Higher Education and Corporate Training. Eds. Rudestam, Kjell Erik and Judith Schoenholtz-Read. 2nd ed. Thousand Oaks, Calif.: Sage Publications, 2010. Print.

30. Bruce LaRue, "Getting Things Done through Action-Learning Teams," *Leadership Excellence Magazine*, August 2005, 18.
   LaRue, Childs, and Larson, *Leading Organizations from the Inside Out*.
   LaRue and Ivany, "Transform Your Culture through Action-Learning Teams," *Executive Excellence Magazine* pp. 14-15.

31. See for example: John Seely Brown, *Storytelling in Organizations: Why Storytelling is Transforming 21st Century Organizations and Management* (Boston: Elsevier Butterworth-Heinemann, 2005).
   John Seely Brown and Paul Duguid, *The Social Life of Information* (Boston: Harvard Business School Press, 2002).
   Etienne Wenger, Richard A. McDermott, and William Snyder, *Cultivating Communities of Practice: A Guide to Managing Knowledge* (Boston: Harvard Business School Press, 2002).

32. Bruce LaRue, "Action Teams Build Momentum," *Leadership*

Excellence Magazine, September 2006, 17.

33. Bruce LaRue, "Developing Action Leaders: Tie Rewards to Outcomes," *Leadership Excellence Magazine,* October 2006, 9.

CPSIA information can be obtained
at www.ICGtesting.com
Printed in the USA
FFHW011930271019
55768269-61642FF

9 781947 309586